Prayer in the Ancient Stoic Tradition

A Preliminary Study with Comparisons to Prayer in the New Testament

Selected Books by Markus McDowell

Prayers of Jewish Women: Studies of Patterns of Prayer in the Second Temple Period

Epistolary Prayer in the Apostolic Fathers

Prayers of the Old Testament: Wisdom, Poetry, Writings

Prayer in the Ancient Stoic Tradition

A Preliminary Study with Comparisons to Prayer in the New Testament

Markus McDowell

Los Angeles | London
www.SulisInternational.com

Published by Sulis International
Los Angeles and London
www.sulisinternational.com

Join the Sulis mailing list at http://bit.ly/2idrJxN

Book design by Sulis International

Copyright ©2002, 2017 by Markus McDowell
Second Edition

All rights reserved. No part of this publication may be reproduced in any form by any means without permission from the publisher, except for the inclusion of brief quotations in a review.

LCCN: 2017903866
ISBN: 978-1-946849-05-2
eISBN: 978-1-946849-06-9
1. Philosophy 2. Religion

All Scripture quotations, unless otherwise noted, are from the New Revised Standard Version of the Bible, copyrighted, 1989 by the Division of Christian Education of the National Council of the Churches of Christ in the United States of America, and are used by permission. All rights reserved.

*To Micah, my son,
who possesses one of the
sharpest minds I have known.*

Contents

_Toc486513608Acknowledgements 11
1. Introduction 1
2. The History and Teachings of Stoicism 5
   History 5
   Teachings 18
   Religion 40
   Religion in Stoic Philosophy 46
3. Prayer in the Major Stoic Writers 55
   Zeno of Citium 55
   Cleanthes 58
   Chrysippus 66
   Seneca 69
   Epictetus 80
   Marcus Aurelius 90
   Summary 97
4. Stoic and New Testament Prayer 99
   God 100
   Eschatology 103
   Human Nature and Responsibility 106
   Ethics 110
   Prayer 113
5. Summary and Conclusions 117
Select Bibliography 123
ABOUT THE AUTHOR 131

Acknowledgements

I thank David Scholer and Ralph Martin, two of my doctoral professors. Dr. Martin led my first doctoral seminar entitled "Writings of the Greco-Roman World." Not only was he an inspiring and accomplished author and teacher, but a man of high integrity and honor. His willingness to help his students find a topic of their passion in academia was invaluable. That willingness led me to focus on the study of prayer in the ancient world. His detailed and excellent work on the hymn of Paul in Philippians 2 was one of the models for my first book which explored the ancient prayers of Jewish women.[1]

Dr. Scholer was my *DoktorVater* and friend. If Dr. Martin began me on the journey of examining ancient prayer, Dr. Scholer helped me to focus that research into

---

[1] Ralph P. Martin, *A Hymn of Christ: Philippians 2:5-11 in Recent Interpretation & in the Setting of Early Christian Worship* (Downer's Grove, IL: IVP Academic, 1997); Markus McDowell, *Prayers of Jewish Women: Studies of Patterns of Prayer in the Second Temple Period* (Wissenschaftliche Untersuchungen Zum Neuen Testament-2 Reihe, volume 211; Tübingen: Mohr Siebeck, 2006).

a lifetime of work. His high academic standards and encyclopedic knowledge of his field,[2] combined with genuine compassion and care for his students, had a significant influence on the direction and manner of my work. His death came much too early, yet he left a legacy that those twice his age would have difficulty matching.

---

[2] See, for instance, *A Basic Bibliographic Guide for New Testament Exegesis* (Eerdmans, 1971); his three volumes of Nag Hammadi Bibliographies covering 1948 through 2006 (published in 1971, 1997, and 2009 by Brill); and his numerous contributions in books and journals to the field of New Testament Studies.

1. Introduction

This book is a preliminary and exploratory examination of a select number of prayers and references to prayer in the writings of ancient Stoic philosophers and writers. The texts in question come from a selection of the major Stoic writings from the period of about 300 BCE to 200 CE: the writings of Zeno of Citium, Cleanthes, Chrysippus, Lucius Anneaus Seneca, Epictetus, and Marcus Aurelius. The selected passages are those that include a prayer itself, a reference to prayer, or a discussion about prayer. Each is examined regarding language, structure, and its content as it relates to Stoic philosophy in general. Since this study is concerned with the influence of Stoicism on New Testament prayer, it does not deal in depth with Stoic writings after the time of Marcus Aurelius (about 180 CE). To keep the scope and limitation manageable in a preliminary study, the primary sources for Stoic prayer is limited to the writings of the six major figures mentioned above. Likewise, I assume that it is possible to speak of "New Testament prayer" regarding some basic presuppositions while recognizing that the situational nature of all the New Testament documents lend themselves to a variety of particular understandings and thought about Christian prayer.

As noted above, this study is not an exhaustive study of the prayers found in the six primary sources as above.

The research presented herein, the examination of the prayer material, and the summaries and conclusions drawn are of an exploratory nature. My purpose for this study is to assess the usefulness and feasibility of a more complete and detailed study of every prayer reference. This would entail a deeper literary, social, and philosophical analysis, much as I did in my study on the prayers of Jewish women in the Second Temple Period literature.[1]

The first part of the book contains a brief overview of the history, teachings and religious views of Stoicism. While each Stoic writer has his own nuances, themes, and emphases, a systematic overview of the philosophy is sufficient for this study. This background material is gleaned from primary sources and modern secondary sources and includes a general understanding of the social and religious milieu out of which Stoicism grew and flourished, as well as a particular understanding of the Stoic view of religion and the gods. This provides some of the necessary backgrounds for reading and interpreting the prayer material.

The second section contains an analysis of the prayer material, arranged by the author of the source material, in roughly chronological order. The chronology has little or no purpose except a convenient way to organize the writers (though a deeper study could perhaps focus on

---

[1] Markus McDowell, *Prayers of Jewish Women: Studies of Patterns of Prayer in the Second Temple Period* (Wissenschaftliche Untersuchungen Zum Neuen Testament-2 Reihe, volume 211; Tübingen: Mohr Siebeck, 2006).

developments of thought as it relates to the prayer material). "Prayer" material as used herein means the text of actual prayers, references to prayer, and prayer language.

The final section examines the possible influence of Stoic philosophy on the language, theology, and use of prayer and prayer language in the writings of the New Testament by comparison of select theological themes: God/gods, eschatology, human nature and responsibility, ethics, and finally, prayer itself.

2. The History and Teachings of Stoicism

History

The Stoic Philosophy, more commonly called Stoicism, was one of the most influential Hellenistic philosophies in the ancient Greek and Roman world, and this primary influence lasted for almost four centuries. Gilbert Murray wrote that "Stoicism was the greatest system of organized thought which the mind of man had built up for itself before the coming of Christianity."[1] Similarly, T.R. Glover observed that it "...remains a fact that Stoicism inspired nearly all the great characters of the early Roman Empire, and nerved almost every attempt that was made to maintain the freedom and dignity of the human soul."[2] This influence did not only last for about four centuries during its peak growth and popularity, but reached beyond ancient antiquity to influence the later

---

[1] Gilbert Murray, *Stoic, Christian, and Humanist* (London, C.A. Watts & Co., Ltd., 1940), 89.
[2] T. R. Glover, *The Conflict of Religions in the Early Roman Empire* (London: Methuen), 1932.

Church Fathers,[3] the *Tragedies* of Shakespeare, European Humanism. It also garnered the praise of such later figures like John Stuart Mill and Albert Schweitzer,[4] to name just a couple. Modern versions of Stoic attitudes, if not the full-blown system, are seen not only in political and entertainment elders but in such fictional sources as the character of Sherlock Holmes created by Sir Arthur Conan Doyle or Dr. Gregory House of the American TV drama *House*.

The early history of scholarship of ancient Stoicism saw the emergence of the philosophy as a reaction to the collapse of the city-state, which had stood for thousands of years as the structure of almost all aspects of most societies. The failure of that model, and its resulting social and political angst led to an ethics of individualism and an "escapist cosmopolitanism."[5] J.B. Lightfoot described this effect as a part of a longer-standing and broader despair concerning the old mythologies, the loss of the independent Hellenic states, and disheartenment with the earlier philosophies.[6]

---

[3] A. A. Long, *Hellenistic Philosophy: Stoics, Epicureans, Skeptics* (New York: Charles Scribner's Sons, 1974), 107.

[4] Ludwig Edelstein, *The Meaning of Stoicism* (Cambridge, 1966), x.

[5] Marcia L. Colish, *The Stoic Tradition: From Antiquity to the Middle Ages*. 2 Vols. (Leiden: E.J. Brill, 1985-1990), 23; see also W. W. Capes, *Stoicism* (London, 1888), 27; Murray, 92–94; M. Hadas, *The Stoic Philosophy of Seneca* (New York, 1968), 20.

[6] J. B. Lightfoot, *Saint Paul's Epistle to the Philippians* (London, repr. Grand Rapids, 1953, 1913), 272.

2. The History and Teachings of Stoicism

Some disagree. Though the city-states had never offered security to its people, the structure of the city-state as a dominant social organization did not change even after monarchs became the ruling powers. So, despite political changes, it is argued that the collapse of the *political* city-state did not, in particular, bring about a philosophic crisis resolved by new concepts. C. Bradford Welles wrote:

> *It is fantasy and perversion to see in Stoicism a new personal doctrine invented to sustain the Greeks in a cityless world of great Empires, for Hellenism was a world of cities, and Hellenistic Greeks were making money, not worrying about their souls.*[7]

Still, something changed. Perhaps the focus was on making money, but this does not mean they were not also trying to make sense of the new political structure. One is not limited to only thinking money or philosophy. New philosophies (or, perhaps, more accurately, evolutions in philosophies) rose to meet the changes in the world. Epicurus (and the resultant school and philosophy know as Epicureanism) pursued one line of thought to address these despairs, while Zeno (and the resulting strands of Stoicism) pursued an alternative view. Both philosophies concentrated on ethics and reflected an individualistic element more than old philosophies. The Epicurean philosophy focused on attaining personal contentment and

---

[7]C. Bradford Welles, *Greece and Rome* (1965), 227.

enjoyment of life, while the Stoic philosophy concentrated on the importance of pursuing virtue and the virtuous life. Both philosophies paid their respects to the waning religions of their day, though again in different ways. Epicurus banished the gods from human life, suggesting they had little or nothing to do with humans—at best, the gods were uninterested in human affairs. Zeno and Stoicism, however, retained the idea of the influence and interest of gods in humans (at least by being present and active) in the world. Stoicism did this by identifying the old gods and goddesses with specific manifestations of the powers found in the physical world.

Some researchers have seen a Semitic influence in the development of Stoicism. Most of this alleged influence is posited to be found in Stoicism's founder, Zeno, and in the third leader of the Stoic school (the 'Stoa'), Chrysippus. Those who have argued for this Jewish influence point, in part, to the fact that Zeno and Chrysippus hailed from the East. A geographic connection might make such an influence possible, but is not evidence for real influence, at least not without correlative corroboration. This led to the further argument that Semitic influence is seen in the similarities in thought between Stoicism and Semitic thought, found almost primarily in focus and nature of the ethical teachings. This is not particularly convincing, as most philosophies or religions which have an element of ethical teachings are similar in both the ethics themselves and the manner in explicating them, even if the grounds of those ethics differ. So, while it is true that the ethical teachings between Stoicism on the one hand,

2. The History and Teachings of Stoicism

and Judaism and Christianity[8] on the other are striking similar, this is no more evidence for actual (rather than potential) influence than is geographical proximity. The possibility exists, but it is not evidence.

Today, for this reason, and others, most of these arguments for Semitic influence on Zeno's thought and Stoic philosophy have been rejected. Without direct evidence, it is more likely that these similarities arise from some of the core universalities found in morality and ethics among almost all human societies, especially during the period in question, at least in the "known" world.

Therefore, the majority of scholars today reject these views and view Stoicism as entirely within the Greek tradition.[9] Nothing in Stoic thought, as we know it today, requires a hypothesis of Semitic influences.[10] "Stoicism

---

[8] Colish, 108. For those who argue for this view, see Émile Bréhier, T*he Hellenistic and Roman Age* (The History of Philosophy, 2) trans. Wade Baskin (Chicago, 1965), 36–37; R. D. Hicks, *Stoic and Epicurean* (New York, 1910), 21; Lightfoot, 299; Max Pohlenz, *Die Stoa: Geschichte einer geistigen Bewegung*, 2nd ed., 2 vols (Göttingen, 1955–59), 1, 22, 31, 66, 107-108.

[9] See Colish, 23–25; E. Vernon Arnold, *Roman Stoicism: Being Lectures on the History of the Stoic Philosophy* (New York, 1958 [repr. of the 1911 ed.), 29–77; Edelstein, 22–23; Josiah B. Gould, *The Philosophy of Chrysippus* (Albany: State University of New York Press, 1970), 18–27; Long, *Hellenistic Philosophy*, 1–4, 10–13; J. M. Rist, *Stoic Philosophy* (Cambridge: Cambridge University Press, 1975), *passim*; F. H. Sandbach, *The Stoics* (New York: W. W. Norton & Co., 1975), 23–25.

[10] See Polenz, 164ff.

can be adequately explained as a natural development of the ideas current among the Greeks."[11]

Primary source material for the study of Stoicism is available only from the Roman period. Earlier Stoic sources are not well-preserved and found mainly in fragmentary records through other writers. No single source remains extant from the writers for the first three hundred years after the foundation of the first school.[12] The primary sources consist of the preserved writings of Epictetus and Marcus Aurelius in Greek, and of Cicero and Seneca in Latin, and the biographer Diogenes Laertius (second or third century CE). Others sources are the writings of some of the opponents of Stoicism, chiefly Plutarch (first century CE) and Sextus Empiricus, and Galen (second century CE).[13]

Stoicism has traditionally been divided into three periods.[14] Early (or Old) Stoa, which remained virtually unchanged from its founding by Zeno of Citium, until Diogenes of Babylon. Middle Stoa began with Panaetius (a student of Diogenes), and is characterized by its attempts to make the philosophy more accessible to educated Romans and to connect it with Platonic and Aristotelian

---

[11] Sandbach, 24.

[12] Sandbach, 18.

[13] Philo is also a source, though he drew on Plato and Aristotle in attempts to reconcile Jewish doctrines with Greek thought. Long assumes that he much of his material came from Posidonius of the Stoics. See Long, 117.

[14] These are admittedly controversial divisions. See Thomas Schmeller, "Stoics, Stoicism" in *Anchor Bible Dictionary*, Volume 6, ed. David Noel Freedman, 210-214 (New York: Doubleday, 1992), 210.

2. The History and Teachings of Stoicism

concepts. The writers of the Late Stoa period show a concern primarily for attitudes towards life and present Stoicism as a practical way of approach one's life. This period includes the writings of Seneca, Epictetus, and Marcus Aurelius.[15]

The Stoic school was founded in 301 BCE when Zeno of Citium began teaching at the Painted Colonnade (Stoa Poikile) in Athens, and lasted until around 263 CE when the last reference to Stoicism as an organized philosophy occurs in Porphry's biography of Plotinus.[16] Zeno, after being shipwrecked in Athens, studied with the Cynic Crates, then moved on to study under other teachers. He had a problem with the Aristotelian dualism between matter and spirit, and formulated an opposing philosophical view, which he began teaching, in which matter and spirit were identical. He revived the pre-Socratic physics of Heraclitus, and rejected the Skeptics' claim that humans cannot possess a certain or precise knowledge.[17] A significant number of young men followed him because he provided them with "a paradigm of virtue in the life

---

[15] Julia Annas, "Stoicism" in *The Oxford Classical Dictionary*, 3rd edition, ed. Simon, Hornblower, and Antony Spawforth, 1446 (New York: Oxford University Press, 1996), 1446

[16] Colish, 7.

[17] Colish, 9. Sandbach, however, points out that in his "…oral teaching and in his written works Zeno must have laid down the outlines of the system we call Stoicism. But it is impossible to draw a firm line between his contribution and those of his successors." Sandbach, 27.

Prayer in the Ancient Stoic Tradition

which he led."[18] Zeno's primary focus was to secure humanity from fear and disturbance,[19] and he thought that the way to do this was to develop a complete system of three branches consisting of logic and theory of knowledge, physics and theology, and ethics. Diogenes Laertius wrote that Zeno was the first to make these divisions.[20] At the end of the fourth century BCE, the ideals of realism had been taught for some time, and skepticism about it has arisen: it had been "tried and found wanting." It was gradually replaced by a new understanding of reason. Naturalism and materialism had become the common ground for philosophical thought. Zeno embraced these grounds in his philosophical teachings—not as exceptions to the rule but following what was generally true.[21]

From 263–232 BCE the second leader of the school was Cleanthes. He was the only authentic Greek of the early leaders, and he took Zeno's description of the

---

[18] Diogenes Laertius, *Lives of Eminent Philosophers*, 7.10. Aratus of Soli was a pupil of Zeno in his old age, and a phrase from his *Phaenomena* is quoted in the New Testament in Acts 17.28.

[19] Everett Ferguson, *Backgrounds of Early Christianity* (Grand Rapids, Michigan: Eerdmans, 1993), 333.

[20] Diogenes Laertius, *Lives*, 7.39.

[21] Ludwig Edelstein observes that when Zeno began his career, the movement of philosophical thought had come to the same place as it would at the beginning of the Renaissance. The realism which had dominated the Middle Ages was to be replaced by a new understanding of reason and of the world. Ludwig Edelstein, *The Meaning of Stoicism* (Cambridge, 1966), 22.

2. The History and Teachings of Stoicism

world and his philosophic view in a more religious direction.[22] His oft-quoted "Hymn to Zeus" describes the Spirit (Zeus) as deserving of worship. The hymn presents the deity as one God, though addressed by many names. Humans are the children of God, and prayers and praise should be offered to him. This, Cleanthes' view of Zeus is warmer and personal than the Zeus of the Greek myths.[23]

The Stoic school declined under Cleanthes, but grew again under the direction of the third leader, Chrysippus. He took the school in a more academic and technical direction by logically systemizing the teachings of Zeno and Cleanthes, making a stronger connection between instinct and reason than the previous teachers. So much so, in fact, that writers criticized him for excessive intellectualism,[24] though others suggest that, without Chrysippus, there would have been no Stoa after Cleanthes.[25]

---

[22] Ferguson, 334.

[23] M. Eugene Boring, Klaus Berger, and Carsten Colpe, eds., *Hellenistic Commentary to the New Testament* (Nashville: Abingdon Press, 1995), 327. For another example of the fervent religious feeling that was sometimes expressed in Stoicism, see Epictetus, *Discourses* 16.25-30. See my discussion on the "Hymn to Zeus."

[24] Long, *Hellenistic Philosophy*, 127. For a more sympathetic view of Chrysippus, see Josiah B. Gould, *The Philosophy of Chrysippus* (Albany: State University of New York Press, 1970) and J.M. Rist, *Stoic Philosophy* (Cambridge: Cambridge University Press, 1975).

[25] Thomas Schmeller, "Stoics, Stoicism" in *Anchor Bible Dictionary*, Volume 6, ed. David Noel Freedman, 210-214 (New York: Doubleday, 1992), 212; von Arnim, *Stoicum Veterum Fragmentum* 2.6.

The following leaders of the Stoa were Zeno of Tarsus and Diogenes of Babylon. Zeno of Tarsus continued the teachings as he received them, and contributed nothing original. Diogenes of Babylon, however, made Stoic philosophy more palatable by his clear and straightforward style of instruction. He followed Cleanthes and Chrysippus in explaining the gods of mythology as each being one aspect of the single God who ruled the universe.[26]

Throughout the latter part of the third century, the Stoics were engaged in a controversy with the Academic Skeptics and the Epicureans, but little is known of those debates.[27] It is with the innovations of Panaetius (185-198 BCE) that the so-called "Middle Stoa" begins.[28] Panaetius' approach was designed to make Stoicism more amenable to the Romans. He gave up the idea of a universal conflagration, became skeptical about prophecy, rejected astrology, and most importantly, focused on the practical aspects of Stoicism practical.([29]This had the effect of shifting the focus from speculative physics to ethics, morals, and social organization, which, in the mind of many, made Stoicism more "stately and enduring."[30] It was during this time and after, in the second century, that Stoicism became well-established as a

---

[26]Sandbach, 115.

[27]Long, *Hellenistic Philosophy*, 114.

[28]Schmekel described him as the founder of Middle Stoa. See August Schmekel, *Die Philosophie der mittleren Stoa in ihrem geschichtlichen Zusammenhangen dargestellt* (Berlin: Weidmann, 1892); see also M. Pohlenz, *Die Stoa* 1.191.

[29]Sandbach, 116; for more details, see Rist, 173-200.

[30]Lightfoot, 276.

2. The History and Teachings of Stoicism

school and a philosophy that anyone could apply to their lives. The work of Panaetius, along with Posidonius of Apamea (135-150 BCE), had a significant influence on the intellectual life of Rome. Both of these leaders severely limited the pantheism of early Stoicism. Many have described this Middle Stoa period as the recasting of Stoic Philosophy in the model of Plato and Aristotle.[31] Marcus Tullius Cicero, a student of Posidonius in Rhodes, based his work *De Officiis* on the teachings of Panaetius.

However, the work and remodeling efforts of the Middle Stoa philosophers did not last long, though their influence did last regarding a focus on practicality. In first century CE, the beginning of Late Stoa saw a return to the doctrines of Zeno and Chrysippus. This time, however, the emphasis was on moral problems. Epictetus and Marcus Aurelius were not concerned with logic and physics or science of the philosophy, but with the shaping of the life of the individual and the pursuit of a proper life lived within the structure of the universe. Practical teaching had won out. "The achievement of what the tradition calls the 'younger Stoics' has been forgotten, and Stoicism ends in a narrow moralism."[32] Some later writers who followed this form of Stoicism have left us extensive writings.

Lucius Annaeus Seneca (4 BCE?–65 CE) was the son of Seneca the Elder, a Roman citizen, and an author. He left his birthplace in Corduba, Spain, to study rhetoric

---

[31] Edelstein, 46.
[32] Edelstein, 46.

and philosophy in Rome. Seneca served Emperor Nero as an advisor until he was accused of conspiracy,[33] and ordered to commit suicide in 65 CE. He was primarily a rhetorician, but he considered himself a follower of Stoicism, and his works reflect the later period of Stoicism. Some his writings have survived.[34] They often portray God in personal terms, reflecting the practical focus of Stoicism.

Musonius Rufus (30–100 CE) was another Roman Stoic who used Stoic principles to answers to questions such as "should daughters be educated the same as sons?" and "what is most important in marriage?"[35] Ariston of Chios, another first-century writer, also stressed the ethics of the Stoic philosophy, to the exclusion of logic. A third writer during this time, Herillus, did emphasize knowledge at the expense of moral action,[36] but neither his name nor his work was as well-known nor as influential as the others.

Epictetus and Marcus Aurelius were the last important Stoic representatives. Epictetus (c. 55–c. 135 CE) was a former slave who studied with Musonius Rufus. Extant works show the teachings of Epictetus to be a "lively, pastoral counseling based on old Stoic principles (with a touch of the Cynic)."[37] Central to his teaching was the

---

[33] Sandbach, 150-151.
[34] M. Hadas, *The Stoic Philosophy of Seneca* (New York, 1968), 10-15.
[35] Schmeller, 213.
[36] Annas, 1446.
[37] Schmeller, 213.

2. The History and Teachings of Stoicism

affinity of man to God. The God of Epictetus is portrayed in even more personal terms than God in Seneca's works.

As Epictetus demonstrated a higher tone of theology in Stoic thought, so Marcus Aurelius on the improved the teachings on ethics and morality. Marcus Aurelius became Emperor of Rome when he was 40, reigning from 161–180 CE. Much admired as a philosopher-ruler, he left a collection of meditations, a personal journal of his reflections and observations on human life and the gods, all based on his Stoic view of life and expressed in practical terms. Many have drawn parallels between his ethics and Christian values, despite the fact that Christians suffered worse under his reign than any other.[38]

The history of Stoic philosophy, therefore, is one of evolution and reaction to the surrounding culture, as with most, if not all, philosophies and religions. The beginning of the philosophy, by its founder Zeno, had its focus on the structure and meaning of the universe, with a call to the individual to pursue a virtuous life in concert with the universe, in contrast to Epicureanism, which encouraged personal contentment and enjoyment of life. Cleanthes brought a more religious view to the school, connecting the philosophy more strongly to the gods, Zeus in particular. Later teachers systematized, simplified, and clarified many of the earlier teachings. The later period of Stoicism saw an increasing focus on individual ethics and morals, and less on the speculative or intellectual pursuits of the philosophy.

---

[38]Lightfoot, 317.

Teachings

Introduction

Of all the ancient philosophies, Stoicism makes the greatest claim to being completely systematic.[39] The Stoics operated with assumption that all things could be discerned by the means of logical study,[40] and they prided themselves on the coherence of their system. They believed that the universe was fully rational and logical, and that the structure could be ascertained by humans. The faculty that enabled humans to reason (*logos*), also embodied the universe at large.[41] Many of the Stoic positions came from pursuing the logical consequences of Aristotelian philosophies,[42] and the Stoics employed a number of Aristotelian doctrines and terminologies.[43]

Stoic thought was not an intellectual pursuit of lofty thought as much as it was a search for real meaning in the world and in life. Stoicism sought to unify all aspects of philosophy. "The Stoic philosophy put Logic first, just as in the measuring of grain we put first the examination

---

[39] A.A Long, and D.N. Sedley, *The Hellenistic Philosophers. Volume 2: Greek and Latin Texts with Notes and Bibliography* (Cambridge: Cambridge University Press, 1987), 160; see also Diogenes Laertius, *Lives* 7.39-41.

[40] Diogenes Laertius, *Lives* 8.83.

[41] Long, *Hellenistic Philosophy*, 108.

[42] Rist, 21. Rist believes that Aristotle himself would have agreed with the conclusions of the Stoics.

[43] See A.A. Long, "Aristotle's Legacy to Stoic Ethics," *Bulletin of the Institute of Classical Studies* 15 (1968): 72-85.

2. The History and Teachings of Stoicism

of the measure."[44] The Stoics drew on the Platonist Zenocrates in dividing philosophy into the basic divisions of logic, physics, and ethics.[45] The analogy of a garden was used: logic was the wall of the garden, physics corresponded to the trees, and ethics were the fruit.[46] Logic included the theory of knowledge, semantics, grammar, stylistic logic, and formal logic. Physics included the study and understanding of nature, living things, divine beings, and theology. In their ethics, the Stoics pursued practicality and not just theory. Speculative physics was the main focus in the Early Stoa, but during the Roman period ethics moved the to foreground as Stoicism became the prevailing philosophy of the practical Romans.[47]

Stoicism also demonstrated a "remarkable ability to assimilate or come to terms with popular religious beliefs."[48] Although Stoicism was basically monotheistic, it was able to account for the polytheistic gods by viewing them as allegorical representations of the one God. In further deference to popular religion, they borrowed

---

[44] Epictetus, *Discourses* 1.17.6.
[45] See Diogenes Laertius, *Lives* 7.39-40. See also Cicero, *De Finibus* 4.2.4; Sextus Empiricus, *Adversus Mathematicos* 7.16.
[46] Schmeller, 210.
[47] C.K. Barrett, ed., *The New Testament Background: Writings from Ancient Greece and the Roman Empire That Illuminate Christian Writings* (San Francisco: Harper & Rowe, 1956, 1987), 70.
[48] Ralph P. Martin, *New Testament Foundations: A Guide for Christian Students. Volume 2, The Acts, The Letters, The Apocalypse* (Grand Rapids, Michigan: Eerdmans, 1978, 1994), 48.

from Neoplatonism to explain the gods of myth, and from astral religions to confirm the divinity of the universe.

Theology and the Cosmos

Physics included both theology and other areas of study, such as cosmology and ethics. The study of physics provided an understanding of who we are and how we fit into the general workings of the world. Since the world is the "substance of God" and God is the "nature which sustains the world and makes things grow,"[49] physics, in the final analysis, is theology for the Stoics and other ancient thinkers. Cicero, in part of his work *De Natura Deorum* (*On the Nature of the Gods*), describes the philosopher's view of cosmic religion from the pre-Socratic period to the modern period (at the time of his writing). He credits most philosophers with attributing divinity to the whole world or its parts: cosmic intellects, the ether, stars, the sky, etc.[50] The Stoics believed that an active principle, called "Logos," "God," or "Cause," and a passive principle, called "Unqualified Substance" or "Unqualified Matter," worked together to explain the state of

---

[49] Diogenes Laertius, *Lives* 7.148-149.

[50] Epicureans denounced this pluralism as a contradiction. See Cicero, *De Natura Deorum* 1.8.18-1.15.41. See also Jean Pépin, "Cosmic Piety" in *Classical Mediterranean Spirituality: Egyptian, Greek, Roman,* ed. A.H. Armstrong, 408-435 (New York: Crossroad, 1986), 410.

2. The History and Teachings of Stoicism

the cosmos.[51] The universe was a giant organism, with God as its life and activating principle, present everywhere, but taking different forms. Thus, human beings are related to God, but are special because they alone are endowed with reason (*logos*), which is the essence of God himself. Humanity's goal is to cultivate this relationship.[52] For Greek philosophers, the word *theos* ("god") in the masculine singular could indicate either (1) everything encompassed by the divine, or (2) to distinguish a supreme God in contrast to lesser divinities. Unlike the usage of the word in ancient Judaism or early Christianity, it did not imply monotheism.[53] (Exceptional humans could be called "godlike" or even have divine status attributed to them after death, or even in life.) For the Stoics, the importance of God as the intellect in the world cannot be overstressed. He is not one God among many, rather, he is the god to whom all other realities of the world owe their divinity.[54] "The entirety of the world and the sky is the substance of God"[55] and

---

[51] See Diogenes Laertius, *Lives* 7.134; Sextus Empiricus, *Adversus Mathematicos* 9.75-76; Calcidius 292-293.

[52] Long, *Epicureans and Stoics*, 149.

[53] Rarely did Greek philosophers deny the existence of gods. Instead, they debated whether god or gods were creators or causes of the world's existence,, what their life and form was like, and what role (if any) they played in the life of humans. All agreed they were superior to human beings in power and longevity, and that they enjoyed a happiness which humans could not attain. See Long, *Epicureans and Stoics*, 136.

[54] Pépin, 415.

[55] Diogenes Laertius, *Lives* 7.148.

"...as gods the world, the stars, the earth and, superior to them all, the intellect in the ether."[56]

The Stoics explained this relationship in different ways. There was a power and a principle which shaped and created all things.[57] This power and principle also unified and gave coherence to the world.[58] The simplest elements are the four (fire, water, air, earth), but fire is the superior element, since the other three are produced by fire and dissipated by it.[59] They therefore identified the underlying fire with Logos and God. This was often described as a "fiery breath," or an "artistic fire" which was self-moving and generative, and the force behind necessity and destiny.[60] This element was variously referred to as "God," "Providence," "Soul of the World," "Mind of the world," "Nature," or "Right Reason." That which holds the world together is the supreme rational being, God, who directs all events for good purposes. Nature and Logos often have the same reference, but not exactly the same sense. Since Stoics distinguished between the meaning of a word and the "thing" that the word refers to, the statement "nature is *logos*" is not a statement of identity or a tautology. The Stoics could

---

[56] Aetius Placita 1.7.33.
[57] SVF 2.937.
[58] SVF 2.549; 1211.
[59] Schmeller, 211.
[60] SVF 2.913, 1132ff.

2. The History and Teachings of Stoicism

also say "nature and its *logos*."[61] This Stoic view of nature resembles the Aristotelian "Prime Mover" as the rational agent which was the ultimate cause of all things. The Stoics also regarded nature as a material substance which pervades all things, and they distinguished carefully between the creative fire (God) and the destructive fire which was an element (*stoicheia*).[62] Yet Stoics also taught the un-Platonic and un-Aristotelian doctrines of the breath (*pneuma*) as the Spirit of Zeus, and the literal creation and destruction of the world.[63] Since they could not believe in a creation *ex nihilo*, they posited an eternally existing substance (*ousia*) out of which the universe arose and into which it would dissolve.[64] They appropriated from Heraclitus the idea of a "cyclical cosmology in which the word repeatedly undergoes *ekpyrosis* and *diakosmesis*—a conflagration and then a reconstitution."[65] This occurs when the planets returned to the fixed position they were at in the beginning. Stoics believed this cyclic repeated ad infinitum in the most minute detail.[66]

In appropriating popular religion, the Stoics made Zeus the supreme god and responsible for providence,

---

[61] Long, *Hellenistic Philosophy*, 148. For a helpful chart of the Stoic ontological distinctions of existence and substance, see Long & Sedley, *The Hellenistic Philosophers,* 163.

[62] Michael Lapidge, *The Stoics.* Major Thinkers Series 1 (Berkeley: University of California Press, 1978), 167.

[63] It was these latter doctrines made the Stoics attractive to the later Church Fathers.

[64] Lapidge, 163.

[65] Colish, *The Stoic Tradition,* 24.

[66] Chrysippus, *Fragment* 625.

creative agency, and immanence throughout all nature. They discarded the aspects of the classical or traditional Zeus which seemed crude and primitive to them. Since Zeus was also the Logos which permeated the universe, it also imparted this *pneuma* (*breath, spirit*) to humans and animals (which were the only two types of beings that the Stoics believed possessed souls).[67]

Knowledge

Philosophy and logic covered a broader spectrum than the concepts of theology and the cosmos. It included dialectic, rhetoric, phonetics, semantics, psychology, stylistics, and epistemology—everything related to rational discourse.[68] The Stoics made a distinctive contribution in the area of dialectic. Chrysippus regarded all dialectic as integral to the whole of Stoicism.[69] Diogenes Laertius lists 311 volumes by Chrysippus on logic, but these works apparently had limited influence in antiquity, which we assume because not much of it has survived.[70] Throughout the history of Stoic philosophy, in spite of many changes and contributions from the various teachers, the Stoics held to the view that infallible knowledge of the world is possible, and that all normal humans have a natural ability to discriminate between truth and falsehood. Formal logic in Stoicism takes its starting point

---

[67] SVF 2.714-716.
[68] See Diogenes Laertius, *Lives* 7.41-48; Plutarch, *De Communibus Natitiis Adversus Stoicus* 1035F-1037B.
[69] Long and Sedley, 190.
[70] Sandbach, 95.

2. The History and Teachings of Stoicism

from the *lekton*, the "meaningful description." It has a subject and a predicate, and the Stoics categorized this structure into nine types of assertions, including questions, commands, prayers, and oaths. The most important category was the axiom statement. This is *lekton* which precipitates truth and falsehood.[71] While ancient critics of the Stoics found fault for their fussiness about logical form and rigorous analysis,[72] the Stoics were not interested in logic for its own sake. It is part of nature, therefore the Stoic sage must practice exacting logic.

The Stoics taught that all knowledge comes through sensation (*aisthesis*) Waves flow out from an object and strike the sense organs. But the soul also sends out the *pneuma* to meet these waves.[73] When this happens an impression (*tupsis*) is made on the soul, like an impression on wax with a signet ring. The result is a presentation, or a mind picture (*fantasia*).[74] The *fantasia* acts on the mind as if on a *tabula rasa*.[75] But the mind compares it to previous impressions, which produces experience, a discovery of likeness, analogy, transference, composition, opposition, and deprivation. The task of education is to organize the mind properly to apply these things in

---

[71] Diogenes Laertius, *Lives* 7.65.
[72] Although many modern logicians find this trait admirable.
[73] Cicero, *Academicae Quaestiones* 2.10.30; Diogenes Laertius, *Lives* 7.52.
[74] Aetius, *Placita* 4.11.1; Sextus Empiricus, *Adversus Mathematicos* 7.227, 372; Cicero, *De Fati* 19.43. Chrysippus explains that this happens to the psyche, but Cleanthes took it literally.
[75] The Stoics believed that at birth the mind was like a blank sheet of paper: it had potential but no content.

daily life.[76] Long and Sedley translate the term *fantasia* with the word "impression," which they say

> *...seeks to capture the Stoics' own elucidation of the term, while it also places this within the modern empirical tradition that they have influenced. The notion of an imprint in their usage gets its particular point from the assumption that any such 'affection' requires a corresponding 'impression' as its cause.*[77]

An impression is not a belief, but only entertains an idea, and supposes no commitment to it. Long and Sedley use the example of a movie: we see an impression of John Wayne on the screen, but not the impression that John Wayne is actually in front of us.[78] Therefore, sensations are real but a *fantasia* might not be. A human cannot control *fantasia*, but he can give assent to it (or not). The clarity of the *fantasias* is the guarantee of the reality and truth. Clear *fantasia* are called *kataleptikai fantasia*, forceful mind-pictures whose truth cannot be denied.[79]

> *Zeno used to clinch the wise man's sole possession of scientific knowledge with a gesture. He would spread out the fingers of one hand and display its open palm, saying, 'An impression is*

---

[76] William Barclay, "Hellenistic thought in New Testament Times: the Stoics," *Expository Times* (1961), 203.

[77] Long and Sedley, 239; See also Diogenes Laertius, *Lives* 7.49-51; Aetius 4.12.1-5.

[78] Long and Sedley, 240.

[79] Barclay, 202.

2. The History and Teachings of Stoicism

> *like this.' Next, he clenched his fingers a little and said, 'Assent is like this.' Then, pressing his fingers quite close together, he made a fist and stated that this was cognition (and from this illustration he gave that mental state the name of* katalepsis, *which it had not had before. Then he brought his left hand against his right fist and gripped it tightly and forcefully and said that scientific knowledge was like this and possessed by none except the wise man.*[80]

For the Stoic sage, it is important not to be distracted by non-essentials. To make the right use of the mind and the impressions were the goal of life. To do so would bring happiness. The Stoics stressed indifference to externals: rationality was the sole source of happiness. It does not matter what happens to a person in life, what is important is that he or she wants the right thing, does the right thing and makes the right use of things. The same was said by Socrates, Plato, and Aristotle—the difference here was that the Stoics insisted that humans must be free from passions (*apatheia*) and not disturbed by external events.[81] This was not an unfeeling coldness of an automaton as the modern use of the adjective "stoic" usually (if not always) implies. An organized and rational person will not be affected by emotions or passion. But through the judgment of the *logos*, an image becomes

---

[80] As found in Cicero, *Academicae Quaestiones* 2.145; see also SVF 2.56; Rist, 139; Long, *Hellenistic Philosophy*, 126.
[81] Edelstein, 2.

faithful to reality, and then true perception comes to the wise person.

The Stoics understood that these concepts were not so simple and clear. But there were some guides one could use to determine a proper understanding of impressions. First, the general consent of humankind, like the universal belief in God.[82] Second, the standard of probability (*to eulogon*).[83] Third, right reason (*orthos logos*) that is, a wise man and his relationship with the gods.[84]

Human Nature

Stoics had a relatively favorable view of human nature. Musonius Rufus believed that humans had a natural disposition towards virtue.[85] Just as the divine Logos permeates the whole universe, so the human logos or *pneuma* permeates man's entire being and accounts for all his activities. Though one is born with primitive impulses, at age fourteen, he thought, one acquires reason spontaneously, and can begin to modify those impulses. Attainment of well-being is possible because nature has ordained that one can do so through one's own power through reason. The Stoics attempted to solve the problem of evil by describing it as an intellectual problem about human will. This was similar to the Socratic view:

---

[82] Seneca, *Epistulae* 117.6.
[83] Plutarch, *Comm Not* 27.9.
[84] Diogenes Laertius, *Lives* 7.54.
[85] See Fragment 2; see also A.C. van Geytenbeek, *Musonius Rufus and Greek Diatribe* (Assen: Van Gorcum, 1963), 18, 28-33.

knowledge is virtue. Evil and wrongdoing are due to ignorance and misunderstanding and can be overcome with learning.[86] Good and evil are antithetical, but are present in opposition to each other, each serving "by its contrary pressure as a prop to the other."[87] Heracles the Stoic wrote that it was not the gods who caused evil, but baseness and matter.[88]

> *The evil which occurs in terrible disasters has a rationale peculiar to itself, for in a sense it too occurs in accordance with universal reason, and so to speak, is not without usefulness concerning the whole. For without it there could be no good.*[89]

Chrysippus noted that nothing is strictly bad except moral weakness. It has been said that, to the Greek, evil was a defect. This is in contrast to the views of ancient Judaism and early Christianity, to whom evil is a defection.

For Zeno, happiness is the goal of life, which he equated with a "smoothly flowing" life.[90] For the Stoic sage, nothing matters except personal tranquility, freedom of mind, and one's own internal calm.[91] Passions

---

[86] SVF, *Fragment* 10. See Abraham Malherbe, *Paul and the Popular Philosophers* (Philadelphia: Fortress, 1989), 130.

[87] See SVF, *Fragment* 1169. See also Barrett, 69.

[88] Stobaeus, *Anthologium,* volume 2, 181.8ff.

[89] Chrysippus as quoted in Plutarch, *Comm Not* 1065b.

[90] Stobaeus, *Ecl.* 2.

[91] Abraham Malherbe notes that the self-sufficient Stoic sage, "secure in the high fortification of his reason and trusting in his

were a psychological form of excitement, due to false judgments about something external. But *logos* can correct these false judgments. Freedom from passion does not mean total lack of feeling and indifference, but rather feelings and emotions within the framework of reason.[92] Seneca includes elaborate examples in his writings of how the Stoic sage can withstand any attack and not be affected, and therefore

> *...girds himself about with philosophy, an impregnable wall that Fortune cannot breach to get at the independent soul who stands on unassailable ground.*[93]

The Stoic view of the political state also revolves around this concept of the Stoic sage. There is no need for the economic or social institutions of the Greek world because each sage is self-sufficient and is of his or her own authority;[94] united to all others by the bond of friendship. Wise people are friends, and true friendship can only exist between the wise. The Stoics suggested a communal way of life, with no distinction based on gender, birth, nationality, property, etc.

---

own weaponry," is very much like the objects of the Apostle Paul's attacks in 2 Cor 10.3-6. See Malherbe, 103. See also Rist, 4.
[92] Schmeller, 211.
[93] Seneca, *Epistulae* 82.5. See 2Cor 10.3-6 as mentioned above. See also Seneca, *De Constantia Sapientis* 3.4-5; *De Beneficiis* 5.3-4.
[94] SVF 3.617.

2. The History and Teachings of Stoicism

Ethics

Ethics was the crux of philosophy to most Stoics, and they stressed that physics and logic should not be studied merely for theoretical interest, but for the light they could shed on ethics. The main object of the study of ethics was to overcome the dualism between the mind and matter as taught by other Greek philosophic schools.[95] The four cardinal virtues were insight (*phronesis*) prudence, (*sophrosune*), courage (*andreia*), and justice (*dikaiosune*). The purpose of Stoic ethics was to show how to achieve happiness, which, for the Stoics, is the same as being morally good and useful to oneself and the rest of the world. It is unaffected by one's outside circumstances. Zeno described it in his formula of what some refer to in modern terms as a *homologoumenos*.[96] Virtue is the only good, and the pursuit and attainment of virtue leads to happiness (*audaimonia*). Health, wealth, and pleasure are all matters of indifference (*adiaphona*).[97]

> *You ask me what the good is like? Listen then. Well-ordered, just (*dikaion*), holy (*agion*), pious, self-controlled, useful, honorable, due, austere, candid, always useful, fearless, undistressed, profitable, unpained, beneficial, content, secure, friendly, precious <...> consistent,*

---

[95] Colish, 23.
[96] SVF 1.179.
[97] Martin, 43.

fair-famed, unpretentious, caring, gentle, keen, patient, faultless, permanent.[98]

Since it was man's nature to be good,[99] moral weakness was treated as a failure to see the good as it is. Perfection is brought about by the person himself, due to the foundation of innate mental abilities.[100] "The most distinctive characteristic of Stoic ethics is its restriction of the ordinary Greek terms for "good" and "bad" to what we would call the moral sense of these words."[101] Long and Sedley write:

The bastion of Stoic ethics is the thesis that virtue and vice respectively are the sole constituents of happiness and unhappiness. These states do not in the least depend, they insisted, on the possession or absence of things conventionally regarded as good or bad—health, reputation, wealth, and so on. They express this thesis by restricting 'good' to what is morally excellent and 'bad' to the opposite of this, and termed everything which makes no difference to happiness or unhappiness 'indifference'.[102]

---

[98]Cleanthes in Clement, *Protrepticus* 1.54.15-55.4.
[99]Stobaeus 1.65.8.
[100]Diogenes Laertius, *Lives* 7.94.
[101]Long and Sedley, 374. See also Sextus Empiricus, *Adversus Mathematicos* 11.22-26; Cleanthes, *Protrepticus* 1.54.15-1.55.4.
[102]Long and Sedley, 357.

2. The History and Teachings of Stoicism

In agreement with Plato,[103] Stoics regarded ethics as an exact science founded on the nature of the world. This emphasis on the responsibility of each person for his state of reason explains the Stoic emphasis on the strength of will and character. The passions dependence on faulty judgments, and this on the perversion of reason is exemplified in Epictetus' writings.[104] Humans have a natural instinct for this proper behavior in everyday life, including an instinct for self-preservation. This manifests itself in caring for others and recognizing oneself in others. Therefore, part of self-interest is also found in looking after fellow humans.

As noted above, Stoics did not pursue logic or physics for the mere sake of knowledge: an understanding of ethics was the goal. As a result, in Roman culture, Stoic ethics became widely known and frequently adopted by people who had no interest in logic or physics.

> *Stoic ethics, were, in fact, easily assimilated into traditional Roman culture. The Stoics preached self-discipline, perseverance, and steadfastness, qualities which had also defined the Roman code of behavior from Rome's earliest history. Stoicism influenced the Romans, but the Romans influenced Stoicism.*[105]

---

[103] But in disagreement with Aristotle.

[104] Epictetus, *Manual* 5; *Discourses,* 1.12.20-21.

[105] Jo-Ann Shelton, *As the Romans Did: A Sourcebook in Roman Social History* (Oxford: Oxford University Press, 1988), 431.

Fate and Determinism

The Stoics, unlike the Epicureans, did not see fate as a blind mechanistic process, but the providence of a god who is Universal Reason. In late Stoicism, we find communion with God expressed in sincere and pious prayers,[106] perhaps the best example (or at least the most widely known, is Cleanthes' "Hymn to Zeus." Yet the Stoic account of the world is still materialistic and deterministic. They described the world as being made up of objects and their interactions. Those objects and interactions occur according to strict laws of the universe. The Stoic view is also strongly teleological: everything happens according to Providence, which is identified with fate.

> *Fate is defined as an endless chain of causation, whereby things are, or as the reason or formula by which the world goes on. What is more, they say that divination in all its forms is a real and substantial fact, if there really is a Providence. And they prove it to be actually a science on the evidence of certain results...*[107]

Since the world is governed by the divine Logos, and the universe is identical with divine logos, it follows that the universe must be reasonable. Chance and accident have

---

[106] Martin, 42.
[107] Diogenes Laertius, *Lives* 2.7.149. See also Chrysippus, *De Fato*; Posidonius *De Fato*, Book 2; Boëthus, *De Fato*, Book 1.

2. The History and Teachings of Stoicism

no place in the Stoic system.[108] The whole world is ruled by God and nothing happens outside of his will.

> *So the good man will accept everything, knowing that it is not only unalterable, since Fate determines all, but also the work of God, the perfect being. Seneca makes him our Father, which suggests that he is benevolent. To repine or resist is then folly, for nothing will prevent his will's being done. One may go along with it in willing contentment, or be carried kicking and groaning, in wickedness and misery. This acceptance of all that happens will bring man peace of mind and protection against whatever he may suffer.*[109]

Zeno and Chrysippus use the illustration of a dog tied to a cart: if he does not walk along he will be dragged.[110]

---

[108] See Aetius, 1.28.4; Gellius, 7.2.3; Cicero, *De Divinatione* 1.125-126; Stobaeus, 1.79, 1-12; Alexander, *On Fate* 191.30-192.28. Most Stoics believed in the possibility of divination and astrology, because the universe was ordered and a rational mind could perceive it. However, both Epictetus and Panaetius rejected divination: the former because it is unnecessary because of man's possession of reason, and the latter because he opposed all forms of religion. See Colish, 33.

[109] Sandbach, 37.

[110] Josiah B. Gould, *The Philosophy of Chrysippus* (Albany: State University of New York Press, 1970), 150; Rist, 126; Charlotte Stough, "Stoic Determinism and Moral Responsibility" in *The Stoics. Major Thinkers Series 1*, ed. J. M. Rist, 203-231 (Berkeley: University of California Press, 1978), 204-205, 222-223; see also Hipp, *Phil* 21.

This raises a question about free will. Chrysippus felt that it was within one's power to make something a fact or to refrain from it. He used the illustration of a cylinder on a hill. When pushed, it rolls, but the pushing was the antecedent. There are other causes at work. The determining cause is the roundness of the cylinder. The same antecedent would not cause a cube to roll. For a person, the exterior world gives rise to representations, but the reaction to them depends on the conditions of the person's psyche.

> *The word 'fate' is used to describe both the relationship of the principal (basic) cause to its substratum (the rollability of the cylinder) and the chain or series of initiating (proximate) causes which might cause the predicate derived from the principal (basic) cause to be realized or*
> *which might prevent it from being realized.*[111]

Therefore, within the structured universe of fate, human action is free and morally responsible, at least from a certain perspective.[112] All decisions are attributable to a person, and in a sense voluntary, and yet a person is never

---

[111] M.E. Reesor, "Fate and Possibility in Early Stoic Philosophy," *Phoenix* 19, 1965: 269. It appears that by the time of Marcus Aurelius, this distinction was lost among the Stoics. Seneca actually defines fate as the necessity of things.

[112] Julia Annas describes this freedom like eddies in a river: although the water is moving inexorably to its destination, eddies within the river can move in any and all directions. See Annas, 1446. The Stoics argued strongly to keep the philosophy

2. The History and Teachings of Stoicism

in a position where he could have done anything different, because of the condition of his psyche.[113]

This view created problems for the Stoics. The famous Lazy Argument states that if a person is sick, there is no point in calling a doctor, because if that person is fated to die, it will do no good. Chrysippus, however, argued that if a person is fated to recover through the help of a doctor, he is also fated to call the doctor. In other words, what will happen will happen, and that is what Chrysippus called Fate. The possible is what could happen, regardless of whether it actually happens or not. Although this may sound like stating the obvious, Sandbach perceptively points out that the concern of Chrysippus was not free will but moral responsibility.[114] In a sense man's actions are in his power, since he can do them, but it is not in his power to not do them. Chrysippus also taught that the gods cause natural disasters in order to punish bad men and warn others. The hunger of the guilty is punishment, but the hunger of the innocent provide them with an opportunity to act as they should: in patience, humility, self-sacrifice, and acceptance of their fate. Therefore, a person is to be praised for acting rightly and

---

from being understood as a system of rigid determinism, they were frequently criticized by their contemporaries for exactly this. See Margaret E. Reesor, "Necessity and Fate in Stoic Philosophy" in *The Stoics, Major Thinkers Series 1*, ed. J. M. Rist, 187-202 (Berkeley: University of California Press, 1978), 201.

[113] See Cicero, *De Fato* 39-44; see also Long, *Hellenistic Philosophy*, 166; Sandbach, 102-103.

[114] Sandbach, 104.

blamed for acting wrongly. Yet these two opposing ideas still seem in contradiction, and Gould concludes

> *...that Chrysippus harbored two incoherent strands of thought, both of which he prized to the extent that he would give up neither, though he was unable to reconcile them. On the one hand, there was the rigorous causal nexus from which nothing is excluded...on the other hand, there is the psychological experience of freedom in thought and action.*[115]

The Epicurean Diogenianus wrote that the argument of Chrysippus was circular: he proved fate through divination and divination through fate.[116] Yet Chrysippus thought that divination was a science, so it did not *prove* fate, rather, it was a pragmatic consideration based on the fact that the world was logical and ordered.[117] Still, it is easy to conclude that the Stoics' desire to attribute everything to a single principle caused a fundamental inconsistency in their philosophy. Gould puts it best when he writes:

> *Such rigid adherence to a doctrine of fate seemed to many thinkers in antiquity a denial of human freedom and responsibility. Chrysippus, as we sought to show, was an equally earnest supporter of human freedom, but, on our*

---

[115] Gould, 152.
[116] von Arnim, "Diogenianus," *Realencyclopädie*, cols 777-778.
[117] Gould, 145.

2. The History and Teachings of Stoicism

> *reading of the fragment, he never reconciled these two views and could have logically sustained them only alternately. Loath to give up human freedom because of the consequences of morality and reluctant to do way with the causal chain because of the consequences for knowledge, Chrysippus has the distinction of being one of the first philosophers to grapple with an intellectual problem that was to perplex thinkers down to and in our own century.[118]*

Long and Sedley suggest that Zeno and Cleanthes may have simply held the traditional Greek view of fate, as the pre-ordainment of certain events or "landmarks" in individual lives and history.[119] Beyond that, or perhaps within those key landmarks, there was free will. In a somewhat different way in addressing the problem, Cleanthes implies that a bad man's deed may be fated, but not in accordance with providence.[120] But Chrysippus rejected Cleanthes' doctrine concerning the non-identity of providence and fate—he wished to preserve the teleology of Plato and Aristotle.[121] Moreover, is apparent in his writings that Chrysippus enjoyed paradox. Sometimes he pushed some of his principles to what seemed like logical extremes. He is reported to have said that if

---

[118] Gould, 160.

[119] Long and Sedley, 394-395. See Diogenianus quoted by Eusebius, *Evangelical Preeaption* 45.3.1; Cicero, *On Fate* 7-8.

[120] See the discussion on Cleanthes' "Hymn to Zeus" beginning on page 69; see also Sandbach, 101.

[121] Gould, 142.

any wise man anywhere stretched out his finger wisely, the action was useful to all wise men everywhere.[122] Many of these paradoxes, for which the Stoics became famous, depended on whether one took them literally or not. So they would say that a wise man is rich, not with material possessions, but in virtues, that which is *truly* valuable. The wise man is beautiful, not physically, but with intellect. The wise man is free, even if a slave, because he is the master of his own thoughts.

Religion

Religion in the Larger Greco-Roman World

In the Greek period, people, in general, turned to the traditional deities when they were in need. They felt dependent on these gods and goddesses, and, for the most part, at their mercy. Moral values were not particularly emphasized, and, in general and with some exceptions, a deep sense of worship or fellowship was lacking. Unlike the God of Judaism and Christianity, the traditional deities did not demand certain moral or ethical behavior, or a type of worship, though they did demand respect. This general world-view changed over time, and the schools of Socrates, Plato, and Zeno all contributed something to that change. Most early Greek and Roman prayers were petitionary, usually in an attempt to influence the gods or goddesses to pay attention to the petitioner in some way,

---

[122]Sandbach, 43.

2. The History and Teachings of Stoicism

or some sort of thanksgiving or prayer in response to some boon granted. This is not to say that people did not have some sense of dedication or worshipfulness to the deities, but it was not usually in the sense of the moral relational and relational "spirituality" that we associate with many modern Jewish, Christian, or Islamic forms of religion.

However, as noted, prayers of the period (that have survived) began to include requests for moral direction and value instead of being requests for physical and material blessings alone.[123] By the end of the second century BCE, we find many philosophical reflections about religious beliefs. There is some radical skepticism about fundamental assertions of religion belief. Much of this was abstract and theoretical, however, and virtually ignored in regular cultic practice. Still, those who taught or learned and followed the philosophic schools did not accord a lot of validity to the ancient and traditional cults. This is not to say that the schools were atheistic or secular—they recognized, to varying degrees, some true rational and natural deity or deities. Epicureans tended to be the most negative towards the traditional religions and criticized particular religious practices. Cynics were divided on the issue. The Stoics, Academics, and Neopythagoreans tend to "accentuate positive theology, alt-

---

[123] Julie Lee Wu, "Paul's Use of Prayer Speech in his Chief Epistles: Backgrounds and Significance" (Ph.D. Diss., *Fuller Theological Seminary, School of Theology,* 1991), 114-116.

hough the leading figures, in particular Seneca and Plutarch, both composed significant critical pieces."[124] Cicero and Lucretius both express dissatisfaction with what they viewed as the degeneration of religion into superstition.

> *Those who used to pray for whole days, and used to sacrifice, so that their children might be survivors of them (*superstites*), were called superstitious, which name afterward extended more widely. But those who carefully reconsidered all things which belonged to the worship of the gods, and, as it were, re-read them, were said to be religious, from re-reading (*relegando*)...So it were brought about that, of the words "superstitious" and "religious," that one was the name of a defect and one of a merit.*[125]
>
> *Do you see, therefore, how from natural things, well and usefully discovered, the reason has been drawn to fabricated and invented gods? And this has begotten false opinions,*

---

[124] Harold W. Attridge, "The Philosophical Critique of Religion Under the Early Empire" in *Principat 16/1. Aufstieg und Niedergang der romischen Welt,* ed. W. Haase, 45-78 (New York: De Gruyter, 1978), 46. See F. Buffière, *Héraclite, Allégories d'Homère* (Paris, 1963); J. Pépin, *Mythe et allégorie. Les origines grecques et les contestations judó-chrétiennes, Philosophe de l'esprit* (Paris, 1958).

[125] Cicero, *De Natura Deorum* 2.72.

2. The History and Teachings of Stoicism

confused errors, and superstitions that are almost old wives tales.[126]

Some scholars, as noted above, suggest that the political insecurity of the Hellenistic kingdoms in the third century BCE contributed to this sort of skepticism and the rise of philosophies like Stoicism and Epicureanism, but this is a highly debated topic.[127]

Religion had a place both in the State and in the home. There was no separation of Church and State in Rome, of course (a very modern concept), so annual magistrates had important religious duties to perform and events to attend and even preside over. This was considered necessary to ensure the preservation of the *pax deorum* (peace with the gods). The leaders of the State must show that the State itself is reverent and respectful of the gods, to ensure prosperity and the avoidance of disasters. It was understood that the prosperity of the Roman State depended on the gods being pacified. Thus we find a strong element of patriotism in Roman spirituality[128] (this is also why many Jews—and later, Christians—were considered un-Roman at the least, and insurrections in the extreme).

In the home, it was common to have an oracle with an image of a favorite god.[129] Household worship was an

---

[126] Balubus, quoted in Cicero, *De Natura Deorum* 2.70

[127] See John Pinset, "Roman Piety" in *Classical Mediterranean spirituality: Egyptian, Greek, Roman,* ed. A. H. Armstrong, 154-194 (New York: Crossroad, 1986), 167. See the brief discussion of this topic beginning on page 7.

[128] Pinset, 157.

[129] Irenaeus, *Adversus Haereses* 1.25.6.

ordinary practice which ensured protection for families, clans, and tribes in everyday life.[130] Public and private worship was an everyday occurrence.[131] A number of relationships between a human and a god or goddess affected a person from birth to death. Parents dedicated a child to a god or goddess by presenting a portrait of the child at the temple to that deity. Adolescents would offer gods the toys of childhood or a lock of hair upon reaching puberty, women offered the work of their hands, and men offered the work of their profession or the fruit from their lands and animals. When a person could work no longer, they offered their old tools of work to the gods.[132]

Due to the polytheistic nature of ancient religion, prayers were frequently addressed to more than one deity.[133]

---

[130] See L. Robert, "Dans un maison d'Ephèse: Un serpent et un chiffre," *Comptes rendus de l'Académue des inscriptions et belles-lettres* (1982): 126-132.

[131] See Nilsson, "Pagan Divine Service in Late Antiquity," *Harvard Theological Review* 38 (1954): 63-69; see also H. D. Saffrey, "The Piety and Prayers of Ordinary Men and Women in Late Antiquity" in *Classical Mediterranean spirituality: Egyptian, Greek, Roman,* ed. A. H. Armstrong, 195-213 (New York: Crossroad, 1986), 208.

[132] Saffrey, 203-204. Roman spirituality differed from Greek spirituality in the tenaciousness of the observance of ritual. Every act must be performed correctly in every detail with exact words. Bronze sheets from Iguvius in Umbria record the precise words of a prayer, with instructions that if a mistake is made, the prayer must be started again from the beginning. See Pinset, 155-156.

[133] Stoics and astral worshippers used simpler and short invocations in their prayers and almost always addressed one deity. See Wu, 136.

2. The History and Teachings of Stoicism

Sometimes an unidentified deity was addressed, and this may reflect the fact that the person praying may not know how the gods wished to be addressed, or the fear of offending a deity by leaving them out. The purpose of much of this was to assure a hearing.[134] The intent or type of prayer varied: a request for benefits (petition) was most common, but prayers were also offered in worship of the gods, and to show concern for country, or for others people. The evidence for thanksgiving prayers is scanty,[135] unlike in the ancient Jewish or early Christian tradition. Confession or repentance were not concerns, even in philosophical prayer. At the most a prayer might include a request to be a better person. However, for some, prayer alone was not enough, and at least in Asia Minor there are confessional steles erected to local deities.[136] Most extant prayers are in poetic form consisting of three elements: invocation, epithets, and then the petition itself. Each element varied according to need. No ending formula is found in Greek prayers, but Roman prayers, especially during the Augustan period, end with a wishful petition for the well-being of the nation, the citizens, the family, and the person praying.[137] The rise of the philosophic schools affected people's attitudes towards the deities and their prayers.[138] The Sophists, Rationalists, and Skeptics expressed negative criticism and doubt in the Homeric gods, but the majority of Greeks

---

[134] Wu, 135.
[135] Wu, 136.
[136] Saffrey, 208.
[137] Wu, 135.
[138] See Xenophon's critique of religion in *Fragments*, 11, 14-16.

maintained their dependence on them. Platonism and Stoicism were the more religious of the philosophies.[139]

Religion in Stoic Philosophy

Stoicism was materialistic, but it was also deeply religious and moral. The universe was not meaningless, according to the Stoics, but purposeful and orderly. The only God Stoicism recognized was Divine Reason, although they acknowledged other popular gods as manifestations of the Divine Reason. A spark of the divine resided in each human, and the wise person will seek to understand the meaning of it, what it requires, and then obey it at all costs.[140] Early Stoics taught that the world would eventually dissolve into fire and purify itself at some appointed time (the Great Conflagration),[141] but later Roman Stoics effectively abandoned this eschatological concept through their neglect of speculative cosmology.[142] In its strictest form, Stoicism offered no hope

---

[139] See Plato, *Phaedras* 279 B-C; *Alcibiades* 2.146A; Cleanthes, *Hymn to Zeus*.

[140] Barrett, 65.

[141] See Aristicles as quoted in Eusebius, *Praeparatio Evangelica* 15.14.2, 15.19.1-2; Lactantius, *Divinae Institutiones* 7.23; Alexander Lycopolis 19.2-4; Marcus Aurelius, *Meditations* 2.14; Nemesius 309.5-311.2; Origen, *Contra Celsum* 4.68, 5.20; Philo, *On the Indestructibility of the World* 90. Boethus of Sidon and Panaetius both denied the theory of the Great Conflagration.

[142] Michael Lapidge, "Stoic Cosmology" in *The Stoics. Major Thinkers Series 1,* ed. J. M. Rist, 161-186 (Berkeley: University of California Press, 1978), 184.

2. The History and Teachings of Stoicism

of personal immortality. Instead, most Stoics shared with the Epicureans the perfectibility of humanity in earthly existence, the corporeality and eventual destruction of the soul. At death the soul was liberated to join the divine fiery essence, the Divine Reason which permeated the universe. Some Stoics held that bad souls perished at death, while good souls might survive until the Great Conflagration. Others had a sort of doctrine of purgatory, derived from some of the views and teachings of Plato.[143] Chrysippus taught that a wise man's soul would survive until the Great Conflagration, but weaker souls would collapse and break up almost immediately after death. Panaetius did not believe the soul survived at all, and Marcus Aurelius thought the soul decayed at death just like the physical body.[144]

The Stoics' view of God is often described as "materialistic pantheism," but it is important to define these terms in order to have a clear understanding of what the Stoics believed and taught. They described God as the ultimate substance of the universe, the "fiery breath" or "spirit" (*pneuma pyrodes*), and its manifestation in the world was reason (*logos*).[145] God is the universe and all that is in it, yet "not in the pantheistic sense that he is

---

[143] Martin, 46. See *Oxyr Pap* 115 about the death of a loved one, where there is no hope offered. Death happens and that is the end of that person in any form or time.

[144] Sandbach points out that the Greek word *psyche* is misleading when translated as "soul." *Psyche* is the *cause* of life, and in human beings sensation and perception, emotion and thought are all part of life if *psyche* is fully present. See Sandbach, 82.

[145] Martin, 41.

evenly diffused throughout all things."[146] God dwelt in the universe as honey dwells in a honeycomb.[147] Cicero, in describing the teaching of Chrysippus on this matter, writes the following:

For he says that divine power resides in reason and in the mind and intellect of universal nature. He says that God is the world itself, and the universal pervasiveness of its mind; also that he is the world's own commanding-faculty, since he is located in intellect and reason; that he is the common nature of all things, universal and all-embracing; also the force of fate and the necessity of future events.[148]

That God is one (*theos* or *deus*) the Stoics borrowed from the Cynics, who, in turn, followed Socrates in this thinking. In addition, they also use plural and abstract nouns for the same concept (*di immortales*, *vis divina*). "This flexibility to speak of a singular 'god' or plural 'the gods' might reflect the deity's multiplicity of guises, but is more likely a reflection of indiscriminate Greek usage."[149]

---

[146] Matthew Arnold, "An Essay on Marcus Aurelius" in *The Stoic and Epicurean Philosophers,* ed. W. J. Oates, (The Modern Library: New York, 1957), 219.
[147] Shelton, 432.
[148] Cicero, *De Natura Deorum* 1.39 (see also 2.12-15); see Plutarch, *On Common Conceptions* 1075E.
[149] Long and Sedley, 331.

2. The History and Teachings of Stoicism

The Stoics advocated an enlightened, philosophical approach to religion.[150] They were opposed to much popular piety,[151] yet they found ways to accommodate the ordinary cult and belief by acknowledging the cosmos and parts of it as minor gods. They explained mythology as a crude expression of the truth: the gods were allegorical descriptions of natural events.[152] The oneness of God was assimilated into the worship of the Greek Zeus or the Latin Jove or Jupiter. Epictetus presents a particular emphasis on the fatherhood of Zeus, traceable back to Virgil.[153] But the Homeric view of Zeus on Mount Olympus was banished in favor of the idea of a God in Heaven.[154]

Zeno appears to have been a revolutionary concerning these issues: he rejected the existing religious systems for his purer system. Cleanthes seems to hold the same principles as Zeno, but finds expression in a more "cheerful spirit"—he is not so critical of the present forms of religion.[155] Chrysippus attempts to reconcile the two views with an allegorical interpretation of the gods, and emerges as a defender of Stoic theology, especially in the doctrine of providence, which was one of the principle teachings of Stoic philosophy to come under

---

[150] Cicero, *De Natura Deorum* 2.28.71.
[151] Diogenes Laertius, *Lives* 7.33; see also Clement of Alexandria, *Strom* 5.11.76 1-3.
[152] Ferguson, 336. Ferguson also points out that no religion or philosophy, including Stoicism, effectively integrated philosophy and religion into a single entity (Ferguson, 574).
[153] See *Aenid* 1.254 *passim*.
[154] Arnold, 222.
[155] Arnold, 217.

attack.[156] He taught that the gods do exist; they are living, benevolent, and immortal. They govern the universe, and they also seek the good of humankind. Chrysippus, and other Stoic teachers, spend quite a bit of time expounding proofs for the existence of the gods. They agreed with Epicurean teachings that the strength and prevalence of human ideas was evidence for the existence of God or gods.[157] The Stoics also argued that without God there could be no speaking of piety, holiness, or wisdom, because the former two are based on the superior character of the gods, and wisdom is the knowledge of things human and divine.[158]

The God of Stoic philosophy is an immanent, providential, rational, and active principle, sometimes identified with nature or with fate. Panaetius said there were three kinds of gods: the gods of the philosophers (the natural gods, which are true), the gods of the poets (mythical gods, which are false), and those of the state (the political gods, which are both true and false because they tie the others together and are to be worshipped for the good of society).[159] The Stoics differed from the Epicureans in that they believed the gods were occupied with matters

---

[156] See Cicero, *De Natura Deorum* 1.39, 2.16, 2.37-39; Plutarch, *Comm Not* 1044D, 1051 B-D; Porphyry, *De Abstinentia* 3.20.1-3; Lactantius, *On the Anger of God* 13.9-10.

[157] Long, *Hellenistic Philosophy,* 267; see also Cicero, *ND* 2.5.

[158] See Sextus Empiricus, *Adversa Mathematica* 9.123.

[159] This concept was further developed by Varro in the first century BCE, which Augustine suggested was the best philosophical defense of paganism for refutation in his work, *City of God.*

2. The History and Teachings of Stoicism

of great concern, and did take an involved interest in humans. In general, the Epicureans believed the gods existed, but they had little or no interest in human affairs). For Stoics, though, God was the designer and agent of all things, and humans are offshoots and partners with God. Therefore, the purpose of a human is to live in harmony with other humans and with God.[160] But the Stoic conception of the divine, even when expressed in personal language, was never the kind of supreme being with which someone might have a personal relationship in the manner of the biblical descriptions of, for example, Abraham or Job.[161]

Hierocles the Stoic wrote that the gods discipline and punish people as pedagogical acts to improve that person.[162] In Cicero's view of Stoic doctrine, every sin is a mark of weakness and instability.[163] "Sin" is described as missing the mark, stumbling along the road, or transgressing a boundary line. There was no place for evil power or powers in the Stoic system.[164] Sin is the appearance of evil, but in reality it is ignorance about the true nature of the world and of one's humanity. According to the Stoics, there were four sinful conditions: fear (*phobos, metus*), greed (*epithumia, libido*), grief (*lupe, aegritudo*), and hilarity (*hedone, laetitia*).[165] All Stoics held

---

[160] Cleanthes' "Hymn to Zeus" gives voice to all these ideas.
[161] Long, *Epicureans and Stoics,* 136.
[162] Jewish parallels always speak of God punishing Israel as a whole and being chastened. See 2Macc 6.14-15; 1Cor 11.30-32.
[163] Cicero, *De Fin* 4.77. See also Galen, *De Hipp et Plat* 4.403.
[164] Cicero, *Par* 3.20.
[165] Arnold, 331.

that all sins are equal because the vibrations in the human spirit are either orderly or disorderly. Rist observes that "...of all the Stoic paradoxes perhaps the most notorious was the bald assertion that all sins (*hamartemata, peccata*) are equal."[166] Guilt is determined solely by motive. The wise man will know when a particular action is appropriate: for example, sometimes it might be appropriate to kill one's father. Long writes:

> *But even in at its noblest, in the writings of Epictetus or Marcus Aurelius, there is something chilling and insensitive about the Stoics' faith that all will turn out well in the end. They were the only Greek philosophers who tried to find a rationale for everything within their concept of a perfect, all-embracing Nature.*[167]

As for religious practices, the Stoics are mostly silent. They did not generally approve of ceremonial aspects of traditional Greek religion, and most Stoics rejected the traditional sacrifices, temples, and images. As mentioned previously, they did find a place for the Olympian pantheon by interpreting individual gods as natural phenomenon that reflected facets of Divine Reason.[168] Seneca appeared to believe that a human could surpass the gods by enduring evils which the gods themselves are

---

[166]Rist, 82-82.
[167]Long, *Hellenistic Philosophy*, 170.
[168] Long, *Hellenistic Philosophy*, 149-150; *See* Seneca, *Ben* 1.6.3.

2. The History and Teachings of Stoicism

of great concern, and did take an involved interest in humans. In general, the Epicureans believed the gods existed, but they had little or no interest in human affairs). For Stoics, though, God was the designer and agent of all things, and humans are offshoots and partners with God. Therefore, the purpose of a human is to live in harmony with other humans and with God.[160] But the Stoic conception of the divine, even when expressed in personal language, was never the kind of supreme being with which someone might have a personal relationship in the manner of the biblical descriptions of, for example, Abraham or Job.[161]

Hierocles the Stoic wrote that the gods discipline and punish people as pedagogical acts to improve that person.[162] In Cicero's view of Stoic doctrine, every sin is a mark of weakness and instability.[163] "Sin" is described as missing the mark, stumbling along the road, or transgressing a boundary line. There was no place for evil power or powers in the Stoic system.[164] Sin is the appearance of evil, but in reality it is ignorance about the true nature of the world and of one's humanity. According to the Stoics, there were four sinful conditions: fear (*phobos, metus*), greed (*epithumia, libido*), grief (*lupe, aegritudo*), and hilarity (*hedone, laetitia*).[165] All Stoics held

---

[160] Cleanthes' "Hymn to Zeus" gives voice to all these ideas.
[161] Long, *Epicureans and Stoics,* 136.
[162] Jewish parallels always speak of God punishing Israel as a whole and being chastened. See 2Macc 6.14-15; 1Cor 11.30-32.
[163] Cicero, *De Fin* 4.77. See also Galen, *De Hipp et Plat* 4.403.
[164] Cicero, *Par* 3.20.
[165] Arnold, 331.

that all sins are equal because the vibrations in the human spirit are either orderly or disorderly. Rist observes that "...of all the Stoic paradoxes perhaps the most notorious was the bald assertion that all sins (*hamartemata, peccata*) are equal."[166] Guilt is determined solely by motive. The wise man will know when a particular action is appropriate: for example, sometimes it might be appropriate to kill one's father. Long writes:

> *But even in at its noblest, in the writings of Epictetus or Marcus Aurelius, there is something chilling and insensitive about the Stoics' faith that all will turn out well in the end. They were the only Greek philosophers who tried to find a rationale for everything within their concept of a perfect, all-embracing Nature.*[167]

As for religious practices, the Stoics are mostly silent. They did not generally approve of ceremonial aspects of traditional Greek religion, and most Stoics rejected the traditional sacrifices, temples, and images. As mentioned previously, they did find a place for the Olympian pantheon by interpreting individual gods as natural phenomenon that reflected facets of Divine Reason.[168] Seneca appeared to believe that a human could surpass the gods by enduring evils which the gods themselves are

---

[166] Rist, 82-82.
[167] Long, *Hellenistic Philosophy*, 170.
[168] Long, *Hellenistic Philosophy*, 149-150; *See* Seneca, *Ben* 1.6.3.

2. The History and Teachings of Stoicism

above.[169] The idea of worship is found in Stoicism in that the gods are honored by hymns (the hymn of Cleanthes being the best example). One does not worship the gods because they need it, but because humans need it to remind them of the existence of the deity. Prayers have no effect on the direction of the world or the will of God, but directs one's influence to the divine within.[170] Vettius Valen (second century CE) discusses, from a Stoic point of view, that one should be disciplined not to desire things beyond one's control or ability.

> *For it is impossible by means of prayer or sacrifice to overcome the destiny fixed from the beginning...What has been assigned to us will happen without our praying for it, what is not fated will not happen for all our prayers.*[171]

Valens had a disdain for the common view of religion that saw prayer as a device to obtain things from the gods. One should have a noble sense of ones' own dependence and role in destiny, not despair.[172] Along these lines, Plutarch wrote, "If you become a philosopher, you will not live unpleasantly, but you will learn to subsist pleasantly anywhere and with any resources."[173] Yet they could not add, as did the Apostle Paul, "I can do all

---

[169] Villy Sørensen, *Seneca: The Humanist at the Court of Nero* (Chicago: University of Chicago Press, 1984), 202.

[170] Edelstein, 80.

[171] Vettius Valens, *Anth* 5.9.2. Juvenal, in his tenth Satire, also treats prayers along Stoic lines.

[172] Compare Phil 4.11-13.

[173] Plutarch, *Virtues and Vice* 4.

things through Christ who strengthens me." Stoic philosophy did not present that sort of relationship between humans and God. However, prayer for the Stoic was not an act of resignation. As is shown in the examples below, prayer was a way to perform a daily examination of the soul, in order to determine whether one was in tune with the purpose of the universe or not, and to adjust accordingly. It was a religious exercise[174] designed to keep one accountable to the goal of living within the structure of and in concern with Divine Reason.

---

[174]Seneca, *Dial* 5.36.2.

3. Prayer in the Major Stoic Writers

Zeno of Citium

Background

Only a few writings of Zeno have survived, and this is mainly through other ancient writers. He was born about 334 BCE in Citium on Cyprus. According to Hecato and Apollonius of Tyre, the young Zeno consulted an oracle in find out what he should do with his life. The gods responded that he should "take on the complexion of the dead," which he interpreted to mean that he should study ancient authors.[1] He also reportedly lived a rather ascetic life. Diogenes Laertius tells of a legend that Zeno was shipwrecked, he went to a bookstore in Athens and read some writings of Socrates, which led him to study with the Cynic philosopher Crates of Thebes.[2] After studying with Crates and others, he began teaching in the Agora

---

[1] Diogenes Laertius, *Lives* 7.1.2.
[2] Diogenes Laertius, *Lives* 7.2–3.

of Athens, at the Stoa Poikile. The name of the location eventually came to be applied to his students: the Stoics.

Later in life he was greatly honored in Athens, and was offered a citizenship, keys to the city gate, and a bronze statute.[3] He was famous for the syllogisms which he used to prove his thoughts: "That which has reason is better than that which has not reason: but nothing is better than the universe…therefore, the universe has reason."[4]

Religion and Prayer

There is not much in the way of prayers or prayer language in surviving information on Zeno. The focus of much of the early Stoa was on speculative physics, not practical philosophy. This is probably the reason why there is not much on prayer, or at least much that has survived. It was left to later teachers of the Stoa to turn the focus to practical ethics and to incorporate more religious practices. This does not mean that Zeno's philosophy did not have religious elements. Though he supposed that a society of the perfectly wise would not build temples,[5] Long notes that this was not because Zeno was unreligious, but because buildings are inadequate for the sacred.[6] Likewise, Epictetus quotes Zeno as having said, "To follow the gods is man's end, and the essence of good is the proper use of external impressions."[7] This

---

[3] Diogenes Laertius, *Lives* 7.6-11.
[4] Sextus Empiricus, *Adv Math* 9.104.
[5] Plutarch, *Comm Not* 1034B.
[6] Long, *Epicureans and Stoics*, 146.
[7] Epictetus, *Discourses* 1.20.15-16.

3. Prayer in the Major Stoic Writers

implies that Zeno had a place for prayer in his system. Further, one of his syllogisms, used often by the later Stoics, was that "it is reasonable to honor the gods; it would not be reasonable to honor beings which do not exist; therefore, the gods exist."[8] Prayer, then, had a role, but since speculative physics was the focus of the early school, little has survived.

One of the few mentions is found in the section on Zeno in *Lives of Eminent Philosophers*, Diogenes Laertius reports that Zeno said "the wise man, they say, will offer prayers and ask for good things from the gods"[9] and "[t]he good (the wise) will worship God, they have an understanding of the rites of the gods, and piety is the knowledge of how to serve the gods. They will sacrifice to them and keep themselves pure."[10]

The scarcity of information on prayer in Zeno's thoughts, and any actual prayers, makes it difficult to draw any firm conclusions about Stoic prayer according to Zeno. The little that has survived demonstrated that Zeno appropriated some elements of popular religion into his system, including prayer. The most we can say is that, for Zeno, gods deserved honor, sacrifice, and one should offer at least petitionary prayers to the gods.

---

[8] Zeno, *Fragments* 162; Sextus Empiricus, *Adv Math* 9.133.
[9] Diogenes Laertius, *Lives* 7.124.
[10] Diogenes Laertius, *Lives* 7.119.

Cleanthes

Background

Cleanthes (331-321 BCE) was the second head of the Stoa school. He retained the doctrines of Zeno, but displayed no great originality except for the addition of religious elements.[11] Grant wrote that Cleanthes was the real founder of Stoic theology.[12] The "Hymn to Zeus" displays a deep piety not found in the other Early Stoic writers.

Cleanthes was so poor that he earned money by drawing water at night for gardens in order to be able to study during the day.[13] He had a reputation of being slow of wit, and perhaps the reason for his lack of original contributions to the philosophy. It was reported that he compared himself to a narrow-necked bottle: it might have difficulty taking something in, but once inside, would never let it go.[14] He has been often criticized for being grossly material, but Sandbach says that this is unfair: "Stoicism is a materialistic philosophy and he was right to try to explain things in material terms."[15]

---

[11] Schmeller, 212.
[12] Grant, 152.
[13] Diogenes Laertius, *Lives* 7.168.
[14] Barclay, 166; William Cassidy, "Cleanthes — Hymn to Zeus" in *Prayer from Alexander to Constantine: A Critical Anthology,* ed. Mark Kiley, et. al., 133-138 (New York: Routledge, 1997), 134; See also Plutarch, *De Aud* 18; Cicero, *Tusc Dis* 2.7.60.
[15] Sandbach, 112.

3. Prayer in the Major Stoic Writers

Religion and Prayer

Most scholarly study of Cleanthes has focused on his "Hymn to Zeus." The hymn generally follows the traditional form of ancient Greek and Roman prayer, but incorporates Stoic elements. The *invocatio* (the invocation or introduction) of the hymn is traditional in the manner of Homer or Hesiod, except for the phrase "first cause of Nature" which demonstrates the Stoic understanding of the Divine Reason. A traditional *pars epica* (the main body of the prayer) follows, which, in the traditional manner, explains why the person is calling on the God, what his relationship with the deity is, and why he thinks he should receive assistance. The *preces* (the conclusion) is the final section of the prayer, again following the typical structure and content of a Greek prayer.

The multiplicity of names for God is not surprising, for it is part of the style of Greek prayer.[16] The reason for this is given by Des Places, that "we know nothing about the gods, nor of their people, nor of the names they would find fitting to give themselves."[17] Since this hymn is the most complete and detailed example of Stoic prayer, we will examine it in detail.[18]

The hymn is as follows:[19]

---

[16] Plato, in *Agamemnon*, writes "Zeus, whatever your real name may be, if this one pleases you, it is what I will call you."

[17] See Edouard Des Places, "La prière des philosophes grecs," *Gregorianum* 41 (1960), 253-272.

[18] For another (non-Stoic) pious hymn from the same time, see the *Corpus Hermetica* 1.30-32.

[19] Translation is by William Cassidy, "Cleanthes — Hymn to Zeus" in *Prayer from Alexander to Constantine: A Critical*

Invocatio

1. Most glorious of immortals, honoured under many names, all powerful forever,[20]
2. O Zeus, first cause of Nature,[21] guiding all things through law,
3. Hail! For it is just for all mortals to address you.

Pars epica

4. Since we were born of you, and we alone share in the likeness
5. Of deity, of all things that live and creep upon the earth.[22]
6. So I will hymn you and sing always of your strength,
7. For all the cosmos, as it whirls about the earth,

Anthology, ed. Mark Kiley, et. al., 133-138 (New York: Routledge, 1997), 135-136. Cassidy notes that there are a number of problems in the Greek text. See the *apparati* in A. C. Pearson, ed., *The Fragments of Zeno and Cleanthes* (London: C.J. Clay and Sons, 1891) and in Iohannes U. Powell, ed., *Collectanea Alexandrina: Reliquiae minores poetarum Graecorum Aetatis Ptolemaicae 323-146 AC* (Oxford: Oxford University Press, 1925). The Greek text can be found in Stobaeus 1.25.3-27, 4; SVF 1.537; see also A.A. Long, and D.N. Sedley, *The Hellenistic Philosophers. Volume 2: Greek and Latin Texts with Notes and Bibliography* (Cambridge: Cambridge University Press, 1987), 326-327.

[20] Note the similarities to some of the Psalms which celebrate God as Creator, for example, Psalm 8.1, 9; 104.1b-2; 145.3. However, the Psalms go on to praise God for his "righteousness."

[21] Compare Col 1.15-17.

[22] Compare Lev 11.20; 11.29; 11.31; 11.42; Ps 104.20; Ezek 38.20.

3. Prayer in the Major Stoic Writers

8 Obeys you, wherever you lead, and it is willingly ruled by you.[23]
9 For such is the power you hold in your unconquerable hands:
10 The two-forked,[24] fiery, ever-living thunderbolt.[25]
11 For all the works of nature are accomplished through its blows,
12 By which you set right the common reason, which flows
13 Through everything, mixing divine light through things great and small.[26]
14 Nothing is accomplished in this world save through you, O Spirit,[27]
15 Neither in the divine, heavenly, ethereal sphere, nor upon the sea,
16 Save as much the evil accomplish on their own in their ignorance.[28]
17 But you are yet able to make the odd even,

---

[23]"Obeys you" means, in the Stoic sense, that the order of the universe is due to the Divine Reason which permeates all.

[24]*Ampheke*. Some translate this as "double-edged." Compare Heb 4.12 and Rev 1.16, which use different Greek words but the same imagery.

[25]Cleanthes (and Stoicism) was influenced by the pre-Socratic philosopher Heraclitus in using the concept of fire as a central metaphor. For a discussion of this issue see Long, *Hellenistic Philosophy*, 145-184, and Long, "Heraclitus and Stoicism," in *Stoic Studies* (Cambridge: Cambridge University Press, 1996), 35-57.

[26]Others translate this as "things great and small" as the sun and stars, but Cassidy feels it best to leave it open.

[27]Compare Rom 8.28, 11.36.

[28]Compare Acts 3.17, 17.30; Eph 4.18; 1 Pet 1.14, 2.15.

18   And to order the disorderly; and to love the unloved.
19   For thus you have fit together into one all good things with the bad
20   So that they become one single, eternal harmony.[29]
21   They flee it, those among the mortals who are evil[30] —
22   The ill-starred, they who always yearn for the possession of beautiful things
23   But never behold the divine universal law. Nor do they hear it,
24   Though if they hearken to it, using intelligence, they would have a fortunate life.[31]
25   But in their ignorance they rush headlong into this or that evil:
26   Some pressing on in an aggressive search for popularity and renown,
27   Others in reckless pursuit of wealth,
28   Others yet in laziness or in sensual pleasure

---

[29] The word translated "harmony" here is actually the Greek word *logos* (reason).

[30] The word translated as "evil" iskakoi« (*kakoi*) as opposed *pornepoi* which is common in the New Testament when speaking of evil as opposed to holiness. See Matt 5.45. 7.11, 12.35, 13.49; Luke 6.45, 11.13; John 17.15; Eph 6.12,16; 2 Thess 3.2,3; 1 Jn 2.13,14, 3.12, 5.18,19. The New Testament does use *kakossin* the attributive to refer to a person or persons, but always in a more general sense than *ponerio*. See Mark 7.21; John 18.23; Rom 1.30, 2.9; 1 Cor 15.33; Phil 3.2; Rev 2.2.

[31] The Stoic idea is that humans resemble God in rationality and capacity for virtue.

3. Prayer in the Major Stoic Writers

29 <.........>[32] They are borne hither and thither,
30 All hastening to become the opposite of what they are.[33]

Preces

31 Zeus the all-giver, wielder of the bright lightening in the dark clouds,[34]
32 Deliver mankind from its miserable incompetence.
33 Father, disperse this from our soul; give us
34 Good judgment,[35] trusting in you to guide all things in justice,
35 So that, in gaining honour we may repay you with honor,
36 Praising your works unceasingly, as is always fitting
37 For mortals. For there is no greater honour among men,
38 Nor among gods, than to sing forever in justice your universal law.[36]

The phrase "first cause of Nature" (line 2) reflects the Stoic idea that all other gods are simply allegories of nature, that is, that they are aspects of the Divine Reason,

---

[32] A lacuna in the surviving Greek text.

[33] Compare Rom 1.19-32; see also Rom 7.14-25.

[34] Note again the connection with Heraclitus.

[35] Again notice the Stoic emphasis on logic and reason as the goal of the human in relation to God, not holiness in the New Testament sense.

[36] This forms an *inclusio* with lines 1-3, thus opening and closing the hymn with praise. Compare Ps 8.

which Cleanthes uses the name of the traditional god-over-all, Zeus. The reference Zeus "guiding all things through law" (line 2) associates law (*nomos*) with Zeus, which is found even in early (non-Stoic) epic poetry, where it referred to the customs of the Greeks. Here, Cleanthes presents the concept as universal and rational (see also lines 12-13), and is therefore an appropriate guide for humans.[37] The following line, "for it is just for all mortals to address you" (line 3) is justified because "by the divine filiation of man everyone is able to invoke Zeus, since he is everyone's father."[38] "For from you we are all born" (line 4) also appears in verse 5 of Aratus Phenomenae, and a combination of the two concepts is found in the mouth of Paul of Tarsus in Acts 17.28.

The *pars epica* (lines 4-30) would traditionally have recited mythical themes in standard Greek prayers, describing the pious worshipper and his or her past sacrifices. Cleanthes states that the reason for his prayer and request is to emphasize that the purpose of following Zeus is simply the relationship between humans and the Stoic Divine Reason. The thunderbolt of Zeus (line 10) was understood as his weapon in the classical myths; but here it is portrayed instead as the "elemental power by which Divine Reason animates the cosmos."[39] This is in line with the Stoics' frequent interpretation of mythical elements of the deities as symbolic representations and not to be take literally.

---

[37] See Cassidy, 134.
[38] Edouard Des Places, "La prière des philosophes grecs," *Gregorianum* 41 (1960), 263 (translation mine).
[39] Cassidy, 134-135; see also Long and Sedley, 327.

3. Prayer in the Major Stoic Writers

In line 16 it is stated that the unwise person is simply ignorant—here is no mention of sin in contrast to holiness, or even that sin, in some way, might offend the deity. Living unwisely, or outside the structure of Divine Reason, is merely a mistake, though a serious one, in Stoic philosophy. Line 19 continues addressing this issue, noting that, although there are unwise people in the world who do unwise things, Divine Reason makes everything work together in an orderly fashion, a frequent teaching in the Stoic concept of Fate.[40]

The closing request (the *preces*, lines 31-38) is also universal in content. Cassidy points out that should not be taken as a indication of the lack of genuineness. This prayer is "the act of a man for whom philosophy is a spiritual as well as an intellectual path."[41]

Despite the sincerity and piety in this hymn, as noted, the prayer is universal rather than personal or intimate, as is fitting for ancient philosophers. The invocation is traditional, and the structure is tradition, but the content of the hymn is completely Stoic. God is described in semi-pantheistic terms, as the embodiment of *logos*, the Divine Reason that pervades all creation and is the source of all creation. The hymn displays the skill with which the Stoics were able to incorporate popular religious ideas and concepts into a philosophical system. There is no sense of repentance or evil, but a request that God help the offerer to be a better person (that is, to live

---

[40]Compare Rom 8.28.
[41]See Cassidy, 135.

within the strictures of Reason as found in the very structure of the universe). Evil is only a human aberration due to lack of wisdom about the universe and life. Still, wrongdoing does not affect the well-defined structure of the universe and time: God harmonizes the bad as well as the good into his well-ordered universe.

Chrysippus

Background

Chrysippus was born around 279 BCE in Soli in Cilisia, where his father had immigrated from Tarsus. When he was a young man he moved to Athens to study with Cleanthes. Around 230 BCE, upon the death of Cleanthes, he became the leader of the Stoic school, and gained much praise for his intellectual abilities. He died at age 73 during the 143rd Olympiad (208-204 BCE). Galen suggested that Greek was not Chrysippus' native tongue, perhaps primarily because his style is copious and repetitive, as others have noted. It as also been noted that his writings on psychology are "remarkably clumsy and ill-constructed."[42]

Under the teachings of Cleanthes, the Stoa had become danger of dissolving into a number of different sub-philosophies. When Chrysippus became the leader, he refocused and affirmed the primary teachings. In doing so, he restated many of Zeno's positions and defined them

---

[42] Sandbach, 112-113.

3. Prayer in the Major Stoic Writers

more clearly. As a result, the work of Chrysippus became the orthodox strand of future Stoicism.[43] He work and leadership was considered so important that Diogenes Laertius was led to write that "but for Chrysippus there would have been no Stoa."[44] Chrysippus was also said to have had the most acute mind of all the Stoics. Cicero considered him to have the sharpest mind of all the ancient philosophers.[45] Having set a goal for himself to write five hundred lines a day, he wrote over seven hundred books. Unfortunately, only a small amount of his work survived, preserved in the works of Cicero, Seneca, Galen, and Plutarch.[46]

Religion and Prayer

Like Zeno, Chrysippus did not have much to say about religion and prayer, for he focused primarily on speculative philosophy (also like Zeno). However, there are two passages (one from Chrysippus' own surviving writings, the other from Diogenes Laertius) which present his

---

[43] Annas, 1146. "The common opinion that he was the source of orthodox Stoicism is probably correct, although it is possible that much of the systematization found in later authors was not his work" (Sandbach, 114).

[44] Diogenes Laertius, *Lives* 7.183; see also Athenaeus, *Deipnosophistes* 8.335.

[45] See Gould, 8.

[46] Some papyrus fragments were also discovered in Herclulaneum at the Villa of the Papyri. See John T. Fitzgerald, "Philodemus and the Papyri from Herculaneum" in Fitzgerald, ed., *Philodemus and the New Testament world Philosophy* (Leiden: Brill, 2004).

view on the proper attitude of a human towards the gods. Like Zeno, he was fond of syllogisms. After reciting a syllogism which proved the existence of the gods, he wrote:

> *There are gods, so therefore they must give signs of the future. If they give us the means, we cannot deny the existence of divination, therefore divination is a reality.*[47]
>
> *Therefore living in harmony with nature proves to be the goal of life, which is in accordance with the nature of oneself and that of the whole, engaging in no activity wont to be forbidden by the universal law, which is the right reason pervading everything and identical to Zeus, the director of the administration of existing things.*[48]

There is not much to be concluded from this and a few other sparse references to Zeus and the gods. Since Chrysippus endeavored to restore and refine the teachings of Zeno, we can cautiously conclude that his understanding of religion and prayer were also similar to the teaching of Zeno on the matter. The gods deserve honor and sacrifice, and petitionary prayer has a place in the life of a Stoic sage.

---

[47] Chrysippus, *Fragment* 1192.
[48] Diogenes Laertius, *Lives* 7.87-88.

3. Prayer in the Major Stoic Writers

Seneca

Background

Lucius Annaeus Seneca is often referred to as "the Younger," or "the Philosopher" to distinguish him from his father, Seneca the Elder, who was a rhetorician.[49] Yet Seneca the Younger was primarily a rhetorician himself, not a philosopher.[50] Born in 1 CE at Corduba in Spain, his father was a Roman citizen and an author. As a young boy, Seneca the Younger went to Rome to study rhetoric and philosophy. He continued to live and study there, and, as a grown man, attained the office of *quaestor* and a senator during the reign of Claudius. In 41 CE he was exiled to Corsica by Claudius for alleged adultery with the Emperor's sister.[51] Eight years later he was recalled and became the tutor of Agrippina's son Lucius Domitus Ahenobarbus (later known as Nero). When Nero became emperor, Seneca was appointed as one of his advisor. As Nero's behavior grew increasingly erratic in is later years, Seneca asked to retire. Nero refused, though Seneca did withdraw from public affairs. He was eventually accused of complicity in the conspiracy of Calpurniu Piso in 65, and committed suicide by command of Nero.

---

[49] He also had an older brother, Junio Gallio, who was proconsul of Achaia for a while. He is mentioned in Acts 18.12-17.
[50] Sandbach, 152.
[51] Probably false charges. See Charles W. Super, *Between Heathenism and Christianity* (Chicago: Fleming H. Revell Company, 1899), 11.

Seneca's philosophic thoughts can appear a bit inconsistent. Some suggest that this may be because he found himself in a difficult position as the advisor of Nero. Others have accused him of being an outright hypocrite:

> *While denouncing tyrancy, Seneca was making himself the teacher of a tyrant; while inveighing again the associates of the powerful, he did not hold aloof from the palace himself. Though finding fault with the rich, he himself acquired a fortune of 300,000,000 sesterces; and though he censured the extravagances of others, he had 500 tables of citrus wood with legs of ivory...*[52]

It is true that his precepts were more noble than his practice. "His fatal mistake lay in trying to do two things that have always been found incompatible: to be a successful politician and an upright man."[53]

Seneca was a contemporary of Paul of Tarsus, and Lightfoot points out that they both "fell victim to the same tyrant's rage."[54] A spurious correspondence between Paul and Seneca appeared in later centuries, probably written as a fictional exercise to explore connections between Stoicism and Christianity. Some early Church Fathers may have taken them as genuine, despite the errors in chronology and history, stylistic problems, and

---

[52] Dio Cassius, 61.10.
[53] Super, 23.
[54] Lightfoot, 277.

3. Prayer in the Major Stoic Writers

the obvious misunderstandings of Stoic philosophy and Paul's theology.[55]

All of Seneca's oratory is lost, as well as a number of philosophical treatises which are known only from references to them. The surviving writings are ten Dialogues, two Treatises, the *Epistulae* (124), *Naturales Quaestiones*, *Apocolocyntosis*, and nine Tragedies.[56] Hadas describes Seneca as having propensities for "elegant" speech.[57] He makes use of every rhetorical device that Greek and Roman theorists had described, but is especially known for his use of the "pointed" style.[58]

Because of his writings which focused on ethics and religion, Seneca was a favorite of the Latin church, and some even spoke of him as marginally belonging to the Christian faith. Tertullian (who was a Stoic at one time)

---

[55] Lightfoot, 271. See Laura Bocciolini Palagi, *Il carteggio apocrifo di Seneca e San Paolo,* (Firenze, 1978), 7-47 for a review of the history and criticisms of this legend.

[56] Until modern times, Seneca the poet and Seneca philosopher were thought to be distinct persons. The only external evidence that they are the same person is Quintilian's ascription of a line from the *Medea* to Seneca. But the internal evidence makes it clear that he wrote the tragedies as well as the essays. See Hadas, 9.

[57] Hadas, 17.

[58] W.C. Summers says that it is "...a kind of writing which, without sacrificing clearness or conciseness, regularly avoids in thought or in phrase or both, all that is obvious, direct, or natural, seeking to be ingenious rather than true, neat rather than beautiful, exercising the wit but not rousing the emotions or appealing to the judgement of the reader." See W.C. Summers, *Select Letters of Seneca* (London, 1910), xv.

called him "our Seneca;"[59] St. Jerome referred to him "our own Seneca."[60]

Religion and Prayer

Seneca criticized conventional religion more often than other Stoics.[61] Cornutus, a freedman of Seneca (or possibly a relative), said that Seneca wrote in order to teach the young not to be superstitious, but to worship in piety. In an early work, *On Superstition*, Seneca criticizes foreign cults, such as Osiris, for excessive emotionalism,[62] Jews for a weekly day of idleness,[63] religion which represents gods in a subhuman form,[64] and rituals which require cruelty or self-mutilation. He advocated a rational mysticism, being conscious of the deity in each individual.[65] All of this, is, of course, perfectly in line with traditional Stoic philosophy.

---

[59] Tertullian, *de Anim* 20.
[60] Jerome, *Adv Jovin* 1.49.
[61] *Ep* 95.47; see also J.N. Sevenster, *Paul and Seneca*. Supplements to Novum Testamentum (Leiden: E. J. Brill, 1961), 26-62; R. Turcan *Sénèca et les religions orientales*, Coll. Latomus 91 (Bruxelles, 1967).
[62] Seneca, *Fr* 35; see also *Ep* 110.7-8 and *De ben* 4.19.1-3. Criticism of foreign cults was common in Rome, but Seneca also criticizes Roman religion. See *Fr* 36 and Ep 95.47.
[63] *Fr* 41; see also M. Stern, *Greek and Latin Authors on Jews and Judaism, From Herodotus to Plutarch* (Jerusalem 1974), 431.
[64] *Fr* 34.
[65] *Ep* 41.1; Fr 123; see also *Ep* 31.11, 95.50, and 120.14, cf. Epictetus *Disc* 2.14.11.

3. Prayer in the Major Stoic Writers

For Seneca, Religious practice is largely irrelevant,[66] but some concessions should be made to traditional practices.[67] His view of religion is similar to the Epicurean view of religion in some ways. Both repudiate conventional notions about and representations of the divine, deplore the emotional "harm" of superstitious excess, and stress external conformity to ordinary religious conventions while being critical of them. Both also use their critique to stress their own more positive view of religion. But Seneca and the Epicureans differ on the content of that ideal, and on their concept of the divine, and the relationship of the human to the divine. For Seneca it is the self where god is found; Epicureans do not believe gods are involved in human affairs.[68]

For Seneca, "error" or "sin" is a failure to attain the ideal, that is, to run counter to the law of the universe. It is never portrayed as an act of defiance to a deity. The principle features of Seneca's concept of God is what one would expect of a Stoic: rationalistic monism and harsh determinism. Sometimes, however, his writings stray from these precepts. To discredit, he appears he is conscious of the dilemma raised by strict determinism.

How can philosophy help me, if Fate exists? Of what avail is philosophy, if God rules the universe? Of what avail is it, if Chance governs everything?... Whether the truth Lucilius, lies in

---

[66] Ep *77.11.12.*
[67] *N.Q.* 2.33, 36-38; *Ben* 2.1.4, 4.4.2; see Sevenster, 84-92 and *De ira* 3.36.32-4.
[68] Attridge, 69.

> *one or in all these views, we must be philosophers… philosophy ought to be our defence. She will encourage us to obey God cheerfully, but Fortune defiantly; she will teach us to follow God and endure Chance.*[69]

This may be why some of Seneca's statements imply a belief in a personal God. The pantheism of the early Stoics gives way a bit to take on a theistic flavor.[70] God is defined as the great creator and ruler of the universe,[71] the god under whose guidance everything progresses.[72] He knows a person's most secret thoughts, and Seneca refers to him as "Father."[73] He speaks of a God who is near us, with us, a holy spirit residing in us. Yet this *pneuma hagion* is not a theological value but a pure physical conception.[74] Sevenster points that Seneca is not serious when he refers to a personal God, and argues that the context of Seneca's remarks show that he is actually referring to Fate.[75]

Seneca does, however, refer to prayer more often than earlier Stoic writers. He sometimes writes in prayer form, and he even quotes Cleanthes' "Hymn to Zeus" at the end of *Epistulae* 107. The opening of the hymn, as shown above, sounds like a supplicatory, acceptance of

---

[69] *Ep* 16.4-6.
[70] Sevenster, 35.
[71] *Prov* 5.8.
[72] *Ep* 16.5.
[73] *Prov* 1.5.
[74] Lightfoot, 296.
[75] Sevenster, 37.

3. Prayer in the Major Stoic Writers

the will of God, but further down in the text it is clear that it is simply an acceptance of fate as a guiding force.[76]

Seneca seemingly had an ambiguous attitude towards prayer. On one hand, he writes that prayer has no meaning if there is Fate. "At most for him it is an edifying expression of acquiescence to ineluctable fate."[77] On the other, he assumes that humans can grateful to god,[78] that God loves humans deeply,[79] and that God is at the service of humans to help them.[80] Still, Seneca's conception of prayer is far more rational, impersonal, and lacking in warmth than these bare, uncontextualized statements might suggest. "When he remarks that the gods are an active influence in men's lives, or that they gave man effectual assistance, he is really referring to the godhead's immanent activity in man's better self."[81] If prayer is simply acquiescence, then there is no point in asking for anything, since all is pre-ordained. Two passages explain his view.

The fates perform their function in a far different way than supposed; they are not moved by any prayer nor changed by pity nor by favor.

---

[76] See *Ep* 107.12.
[77] Sevenster, 44.
[78] See *Ep* 15.10.
[79] *Prov* 2.6.
[80] *Ep* 95.17.
[81] Sevenster, 43

Prayer in the Ancient Stoic Tradition

> *Their course is irrevocable; once they have entered upon it they flow on by unalterable decree.*[82]
>
> *...it is foolish to pray for this [sound understanding] when you can acquire it for yourself. We do not need to uplift our hands towards heaven, or beg the keeper of the temple to let us approach his idol's ear, as if in this way out prayers were most likely to be heard. God is near you, he is with you, he is within you.*[83]

Sevenster notes that Seneca is not condemning prayer itself, but hasty use of it by persons who are not willing to exert themselves. One might expect Seneca to abandon prayer altogether, yet he does not. He urges a

> *...prayer for a sound mind and for good health...and of course you should offer these prayers frequently. Call boldly upon God; you will not be asking him for that which belongs to another.*[84]

It is not dishonorable to make supplications to the gods.[85] One should beg the gods to realize their promises, and ask them to stave off threats.[86] To people who say the gods are unconcerned with the world, Seneca responds:

---

[82] *N.Q.* 2.35.1-2.
[83] *Ep* 41.1; cf. *N.Q.* 3. praef. 14; *Ep* 95.50.
[84] *Ep* 10.4; see also 31.2.
[85] *Ben* 2.1.4.
[86] *N.Q.* 2.33.

3. Prayer in the Major Stoic Writers

> *He who says this does not hearken to the voices of those who pray and of those who all around him, lifting up their hands to heaven, offering vows for blessings public and private. Assuredly this would not be the case, assuredly all mortals would not have agreed upon this madness of addressing divinities that were deaf and gods that were ineffectual, unless we were conscious of their benefits that are sometimes presented unasked, sometimes are granted in answer to prayer — great and timely gifts, which by their coming remove grave menaces.*[87]

In *Naturales Quaestiones*, Seneca struggles with these competing concepts. He writes that, if there is Fate, everything proceeds according to a plan: therefore there is no place for prayer. But if prayer is understood as the starting point, then the course of events might be altered by prayer. In that case, Fate does not reign inexorably. Sevenster notes "It may be observed that it is precisely in this book that Seneca clings most tenaciously to the idea of the indissolubility of the bonds of Fate."[88] Yet Seneca sees prayer as "openings in the chain of events which may be filled in various ways. If this is so, then the iron rule of destiny is disturbed. Then there is apparently something on which fate has no hold."[89] The fixed

---

[87]*Ben* 4.4.2.
[88]Sevenster, 46. See *N.Q.* 2.35.1-2.
[89]Sevenster, 48.

course of events *could* be altered by prayer at certain moments.

> *Some things are in fact left by the immortal gods in such a state of suspense as to turn to the advantage of worshippers if they employ prayer to heaven and take vows upon them.*[90]

Apparently, this means that one can be an instrument of fate through prayer. Prayer becomes part of the consequence of events. "Accordingly prayer can be no more than a cog in the tremendous mechanism of ineluctable destiny."[91]

When we compare the writings of Seneca to the New Testament, there are striking parallels—more so than in most other Stoic writers. Lightfoot notes many parallels between the moral teachings of the Sermon on the Mount and Seneca's moral teachings,[92] and points out that the coincidences with the language of Paul are even more numerous and striking.[93] It is this which has led later writers to suppose an interaction between Paul and Seneca.[94] Yet many of these coincidences are also found between Seneca and other, non-Christians writers. The

---

[90] *N.Q.* 2.37.2.
[91] Sevenster, 49. cf. de Bovis, p 205: "un des mécanismes de la Nécessité Universelle."
[92] See Lightfoot, 283-285.
[93] See Lightfoot, 287-290.
[94] This was a favorite subject of French writers. A. Fleury, *Saint Paul et Sénèque* (Paris, 1853) tried to show Seneca was a disciple of Paul. More critical is C. Aubertin, *Etude Critique sur les rapparts supposés entre Sénèque et Saint Paul* (Paris, 1857).

3. Prayer in the Major Stoic Writers

similarities are more likely because of the pervasive cultural ideas and the language of the time, and does not constitute actual and direct connections.[95] Charles Super writes (of Seneca's work) that

> ...*his philosophy and morality show, in a striking way, that a man may approach very close to the boundary line of Christianity without crossing it; without even knowing what is before him.*[96]

While the previous quote is a bit questionable because it reads Christianity into Seneca when he may not even have been aware of its existence, it does show that Christianity reflects the culture and language of the time in which it grew. Likewise, Seneca reflects many of those concepts. His basic view of religion and prayer are Stoic, not Christian. Sevenster, discussing Seneca's view of God, states it well:

> *When all is said and done, fate, nature, and his deeds are the decrees of fate, the enactment of the laws of nature. 'God' or 'gods' are ultimately nothing but figuratively used, friendly terms for the irresistible fate, for which man is no match, and to which he voluntarily submits, if he has any wisdom.*[97]

Perhaps the last word lies with Seneca himself:

---

[95] See Lightfoot, 293-294.
[96] Super, 56.
[97] Sevenster, 39.

...for there is not Nature without God, not God without Nature, but both are the same things, they differ only in their function.[98]

Epictetus

Background

Epictetus lived from 55-135 CE. He was originally a slave from Phrygia, and served Nero's freedman and secretary Epaphroditos. His master allowed him to study Stoic philosophy under Musonius Rufus. At some point of after the death of Nero, he was manumitted, and he began teaching Stoicism in Rome. When Domitian banished all philosophers from Rome in 89 CE, Epictetus set up a school in Nicopolis, Greece. Marcus Aurelius, later to become Emperor of Rome, was a student of Epictetus. Another student, Arrian, published his teachings under the title *Discourses*, four books of which survive. P.E. Matheson wrote:

It is a striking testimony to the wide range of Stoic influence that it should have found its highest expression in a Roman Emperor [Marcus Aurelius] and a Greek Slave, both finding

---

[98] *Ben* 4.8.1-2.

3. Prayer in the Major Stoic Writers

> *common ground in the Stoic doctrine and the language of the later Greek world.[99]*

The merits of the writings of Epictetus were recognized positively by Christians such as Chrysostom, Gregory of Nazianzen, Augustine, and Origen.

Religion and Prayer

The religious elements within Stoicism are explorer more fully by Epictetus than any other representative of the school. For Epictetus, all things, even apparent evils, are the will of God and part of his universal plan, and therefore good. He viewed the universe as a great government made up of humans and God. All rational beings were derived from God's being. Therefore, everyone was a citizen and should be in communion with one another. Epictetus was devout, grateful, and humble—there is not much of the exultation of self that is common in many other Stoic writers.[100]

Like all Stoics, Epictetus taught that disbelief in the gods was foolishness.

> *...take the mere fact that milk is produced from grass and cheese from milk and wool from skin. Who is it that has created or devised these*

---

[99] P. E. Matheson, *Epictetus, The Discourses and Manual*, (Oxford, 1916), 13.

[100] See Seneca, *De Prov* 6.6.

things? 'No one', he says. Oh the depth of man's stupidity and shamelessness![101]

It can be readily seen that, despite his deep religious sense, he is a Stoic through and through. A sense of his view of God, and of prayer through the lens of Stoic philosophy is readily seen in his own writings.

> *Are they not [the gods] at the same distance from everywhere? Do they not everywhere equally see what is happening?*[102]
>
> *What then, is the true nature of God? Flesh? Far from it! Land? Far from it! Fame? Far from it! It is intelligence, knowledge, right reason.*[103]
>
> *Zeus has ordained that there be summer and winter, plenty and poverty, virtue and vice and all such opposites for the sake of the harmony of the whole.*[104]

Epictetus believed that the purpose of life was to be in harmony with God. If a person wanted to be content in life, they should ask "…how may I follow the gods in everything, and how may I be acceptable to the divine administration, and how may I become free?"[105] The sense of Stoic determinism is also found often in his writings: "Whenever you find fault with the Providences,

---

[101] Epictetus, *Discourses* 1.16.1-8.
[102] Epictetus, *Discourses* 4.4.48. Compare Matt 24.36.
[103] Epictetus, *Discourses* 2.8.2.
[104] Epictetus, *Discourses* 1.12.16.
[105] Epictetus, *Discourses* 1.12.8.

only consider and you will recognize that what happens is in accordance with reason."[106]

Epictetus emphasized the importance of the proper understanding of the divine as basic to proper piety.

> *On piety towards the gods, I would have you know, the chief element is this, to have right opinions about them—as existing and as administering the universe well and justly—and to have set yourself to obey them, and to submit to everything that happens, and to follow it voluntarily, in the belief that it is being fulfilled by the highest intelligence.*[107]

He did not criticize popular religion as much as previous Stoic philosophers. He encouraged acts of piety, and even taught that sacrifices were acceptable, if done in moderation.

> *But it is always appropriate to make libations, and sacrifices, and to give of the first fruits after the manner of our fathers, and to do all this with purity, and not in a slovenly or careless fashion, not, indeed, in a niggardly way, not yet beyond our means.*[108]
>
> *Now whoever sacrificed as a thank-offering for having had right desire, or for having exercised choice in accordance with nature? For*

---

[106]Epictetus, *Discourses* 3.17.1.
[107]Epictetus, *Encheiridion* 31.
[108]Epictetus, *Encheiridion* 31.

we give thanks to the gods for that wherein we set the good.[109]

He often refers to God in personal ways, calling him "Father" in a number of places. "I may not rightfully dishonor a father, no even worse a man that art thou should come; for Zeus, the God of fathers, are they all,"[110] and "...a servant of Zeus, who is father of us all."[111] No other Stoic writer displays as strong a spirit of piety as Epictetus.

When you come into the presence of some prominent man, remember that Another looks from above on what is taking place, and that you must please Him rather than this man.[112]
Remember God, call upon him as helper (bo-ethon) and protector, as the sailors call upon Castor and Pollux in a storm.[113]

This collection of his own writings show his strong sense of Stoic religion, and, as might be expected, his writings also include much about prayer. Epictetus' teachings contain far more prayers and references to prayer than

---

[109] Epictetus, *Discourses* 1.19.25. See also 4.6.31-32.

[110] Epictetus, *Discourses* 3.11.5.

[111] Epictetus, *Discourses* 3.22.82. See also 3.24.3, 16. Notice that these references all mention God as Zeus, who is called the father of mankind in traditional religion as well as here and in Christian writings.

[112] Epictetus, *Discourses* 1.30.1.

[113] Epictetus, *Discourses* 2.18.29. Compare Rom 10.13, which uses same word for "calling upon" God, and Heb 13.6, which uses same word for 'helper.'

any other Stoic writer, including injunctions to pray, instructions on how and what to pray, as well as actual prayers. Many of these references are to petitionary prayer, the most common form of prayer in the ancient world. yet they also display the characteristic piety so common in Epictetus. It is no wonder early Christians found the writings of Epictetus amenable.

> *Has not Zeus given you directions? Has he not given you that which is your own, unhindered and unrestrained, while that which is not your own is subject to hindrance and restraint?*[114]
>
> *But give them to Zeus and the other gods; entrust them to their keeping, let them exercise the control; let your desire and your aversion be ranged on their side—and how can you be troubled any longer?*[115]
>
> *To look up into heaven as the Friend of God* (philon tou theou) *fearing nothing of the things that can happen.*[116]

Epictetus also encourages prayers of praise:

> *Was it not god who brought you in? Did he not show you the light? Did he not give you fellow-workers, and senses, and reason?...Are you not willing then, for as long as is granted you, to*

---

[114] Epictetus, *Discourses* 1.24.3. See also 1.25.5-6.
[115] Epictetus, *Discourses* 2.17-25-26.
[116] Epictetus, *Discourses* 2.17.29. Compare James 2.2; John 15.14.

> *observe the procession and the festival, and then, when he brings you out, to go with reverence and thanks for what you have heard and seen?*[117]

Nay, what language is adequate to praise them all or bring them home to our minds as they deserve? Why, if we had sense, ought we to be doing anything else, publicly and privately, than hymning and praising the Deity, and rehearsing His benefits? Ought we not, as we dig and laugh and eat, to sing the hymn of praise to God. 'Great is God, that He hath furnished us these instruments wherewith we shall till the earth. Great is God, that He hath given us hands, and power to swallow, and a belly, and power to grow unconsciously, and to breath while asleep.' This is what we ought to sing on every occasion, and above all to sing the greatest and divinest hymn, that God has given us the faculty to comprehend these things and to follow the path of reason...If indeed, I were a nightingale, I should be singing as a nightingale; if a swan, as a swan. But as it is, I am a rational being, therefore I must be singing hymns of praise to God. Thus is my task; I do it, and will not desert this post, as long as it may be given me to fill it; and I exhort you to join me in this same song.[118]

Many of the prayers of Epictetus reflect, on the surface, a sense of devotion to God and whatever he wills. But underlying that surface characteristic still lies the

---

[117] Epictetus, *Discourses* 4.1.104-105.
[118] Epictetus, *Discourses* 1.16.15-21. See also 3.26.29-30.

3. Prayer in the Major Stoic Writers

Stoic view of Fate and determinism. Epictetus' understanding of those Stoic doctrines is just as strong as any other Stoic writer.

> *Be bold to look towards God and say, "Use me henceforth for whatever Thou wilt; I am of one mind with Thee; I am Thine; I crave exemption from nothing that seems good in thy sight; where Thou wilt, lead me in what raiment Though wilt, clothe me. Wouldst Thou have me to hold office, or remain in private life; to remain here or go into exile; to be poor or be rich? I will defend all these Thy acts before men...*[119]
>
> *In a word will nothing else but what God wills.*[120]
>
> *For what God wills I consider better than what I will.*[121]

Epictetus, like other Stoic writers, quotes lines from Cleanthes' "Hymn to Zeus," and often includes the prayer "Lead thou me on, O Zeus, and Destiny."[122] This demonstrates his dedication to the Stoic idea of determinism, and the fact that the sage is free from fear because he is living in harmony with nature. "[H]e will be free, serene, happy, unharmed, high-minded, reverent, giving thanks

---

[119] Epictetus, *Discourses* 2.16.41-43.
[120] Epictetus, *Discourses* 2.17.22.
[121] Epictetus, *Discourses* 4.7.20; see also 2.7.13, 2.16.42, 4.7.20, Compare Acts 21.14; Eph 6.6-7.
[122] Epictetus, *Discourses* 2.18.42; 3.22.95; see also 3.22.85; 4.1.131; 4.4.34; *Encheiridion* 53.

for all things to God, under no circumstances finding fault with anything that has happened..."[123] "For the only thing that is under your control—the proper use of impressions."[124]

The Stoic concept that Reason pervades the universe is also found in Epictetus' writings. He speaks of humans as being descended from God,[125] and of God as their father, but he also expresses some of the more pantheistic views of Stoicism.

> *When you have shut your doors and made it dark within, remember never to say that you are alone; for you are not, but God is within and your genius (*daimon*).*[126]
>
> *It is in thyself that thou dost carry him (God) and thou dost not perceive that thou profanest Him by unclean thought and impure actions...and when God himself is within you and sees and hears everything.*[127]
>
> *Will you not bear in mind, whenever you eat, who you are that eat, and whom you are nourishing? Whenever you indulge in intercourse*

---

[123] Epictetus, *Discourses* 4.7.9.
[124] Epictetus, *Discourses* 1.12.34. See also 1.12.25-26; 1.9.24-26; 4.10.14-16; *Fragment* 4.
[125] Epictetus, *Discourses* 1.3.1-3; 1.9.6, 13; compare Luke 3.23, 38; Matt 6.4ff; Eph 4.6; 1 Cor 11.7.
[126] Epictetus, *Discourses* 1.14.13, 14.
[127] Epictetus, *Discourses* 2.8.13-14. Compare 1 Cor 6.15, 19; Eph 4.30.

3. Prayer in the Major Stoic Writers

with women, whom you are that do this? Whenever you mix in society, whenever you take of physical exercise, or engage in conversation, do you not know that is God you are nourishing and training? You bear God about with you, poor wretch, and know it not. Do you think I speak of some external god of silver and gold? No, you bear him about within you, and you are unaware that you are defiling him with unclean thoughts and foul actions. If an image of God were present, you would not dare do to any of the things you; yet when God himself is present within you and sees and hears all things, you are not ashamed of thinking and acting thus: O slow to understand you nature, and estranged from God![128]

The number of prayers and especially the language used have led some to suggest that Epictetus was familiar with Christianity, and was expressing, or co-opting, some of those ideas. But, as in Seneca, when read in context these statements are still fundamentally Stoic. The language may be similar to New Testament language, but the content is based on the Stoic concepts of Fate, monotheistic pantheism, and materialistic theology. Perhaps he was influenced by Christian language, or perhaps such language was simply in the air of the culture, and Christianity and Epictetus adopted it. Whatever the influence, or lack, Stoic prayer is still in its own category. Epictetus'

---

[128] Epictetus, *Discourses* 2.8.9-14.

contribution was to infuse it with a more personal sense of piety and religiosity.

Marcus Aurelius

Background

Marcus Aurelius was born in 121 CE to a prominent family in Rome. He was the nephew of Emperor Antoninius' wife, and adopted by grandfather Marcus Annius Verus II after his father died. He was trained in rhetoric and philosophy, but abandoned the studies of rhetoric when he was twenty-five. When Hadrian became ill, he appointed Aurelius Antoninus to succeeded him, but with the condition that he adopt Marcus. Though Marcus was not happy with this, perhaps mainly because it took him away from his prime focus on studies, it did lead to him holding positions such as *quaestor* and consul positions. As much as he could, he continued to pursue his philosophical education. At Antoninius' death, he became the leader of Rome along with his adoptive brother Lucius, but Marcus had the greater authority, and eventually became Emperor.

During his reign as Emperor he was faced with the problem of barbarian raiders along the borders of the Empire. There was also quite a bit of persecution of

Christians during his rule. Long and Sandbach do not believe he authorized these pogroms.[129] Matthew Arnold, however, writes:

> ...[t]he Antonines lived and died with an utter misconception of Christianity; Christianity grew up in the Catacombs, not in Palestine. And Marcus Aurelius incurs no moral reproach by having authorized the punishment of the Christians; he does not thereby become in the least what we mean by persecutor. One may concede that it was impossible for him to see Christianity for what it really was...[130]

Other sources suggest that he was a thoughtful, lenient Emperor. His writings which have survived were not intended for publication—they are a private journal of meditations. Reflective of Roman Stoicism, near the end of its existence as a practiced philosophy, these meditations mostly address ethics and practicality. There is very little discussion of speculative physics, and little about religion or prayer. While this might be due to the nature of the writings—meditations—it is also apparent, in its historical context, that Stoicism has become a philosophy for the practical Roman world. "The sentences of Seneca are stimulating to the intellect; the sentences of Epictetus are fortifying to the character; the sentences of Marcus Aurelius find their way to the soul."[131]

---

[129]Sandbach, 172.
[130]Arnold, 602.
[131]Arnold, 604.

Religion and Prayer

Marcus Aurelius does not write much about religion or include many references to prayer. The *Meditations* are mostly random reflections. They often portray the moodiness and somber reflection of a man's private thoughts. Marcus believed the goal of life for rational beings was to "submit themselves to the reason and law of that archetypal city and polity—the Universe."[132] Like other Stoics, he was adamant about the existence of the gods. "Nay, but there are Gods, and they do concern themselves with human beings; and they have put it wholly in man's power not to fall into evils that are truly such."[133] He believed them to be immortal, and following the gods was the most important thing a human could do.[134] His view of Fate and Necessity are also the standard Stoic teachings and beliefs.

> *Full of Providence are the works of the Gods, not are Fortune's works independent of Nature or of the woven texture and interlacement of all that is under the control of Providence. Thence are all things derived; but Necessity too plays its part and the Welfare of the whole Universe of which thou are a portion.*[135]
>
> *If then there be an inevitable Necessity, why kick against the pricks? If Providence that is*

---

[132] Marcus Aurelius, *Meditations* 2.16.
[133] Marcus Aurelius, *Meditations* 2.11.
[134] Marcus Aurelius, *Meditations* 6.7; 7.31; 9.37.
[135] Marcus Aurelius, *Meditations* 2.3.

> *ready to be gracious, render thyself worthy of divine succor.*[136]

Marcus Aurelius' attitude towards Fate is almost unfeeling. He does not seem to struggle with the problem of free will versus fate, as Seneca did, nor does he portray fate in terms of deep piety as found in the writings of Epictetus. Instead, Marcus urges each person to welcome everything that happens, even if it is harsh, because it contributes to the universe and is advantageous to the whole rational world. A human is simply a cog in the machine of the universe.

> *Provided I remember that I am part of this kind of whole, I shall be content with all that happens. And so far as I am in a relationship of kinship with the parts like myself, I shall do nothing unsociable...*[137]

Marcus Aurelius is fond of urging as a motive for man's cheerful acquiescence in whatever befalls him, that "whatever happens to every man is for the interest of the universal," that the whole contains nothing which is not for its advantage that everything which happens to a man is to be accepted, "even if it seems disagreeable, because it leads to the health of the universe." And the whole

---

[136] Marcus Aurelius, *Meditations* 12.14.

[137] Marcus Aurelius, *Meditations* 10.6. See also Long, *Hellenistic Philosophy*, 180; Long, *Epicureans and Stoics*, 149.

course of the universe, he adds, has a providential reference to man's welfare: "all other things have been made for the sake of rational beings."[138]

The ruling reason of the universe also dwells in humans. This is not simply for justice, but also for piety and the service of God.[139] Marcus Aurelius does not discuss popular religion, although he does assume that one will pray and offer sacrifices. The Stoic version of pantheistic monism is evident in his writings.

> *Walk with the Gods! And he does walk with the Gods, who lets them see his soul invariably satisfied with its lot and carrying out the will of that 'genius,' a particle of himself, which Zeus has given to every man as his captain and guide—and this is none other than each man's intelligence and reason.*
>
> *Cease not to think of the Universe as one living Being, possessed of a single Substance and a single Soul; and how all things trace back to its single sentience; and how it does all things by a single impulse; and to all existing things are joint causes of all things that come into existence; and how intertwined in the fabric is the thread and how closely woven the web.*[140]

---

[138] Arnold, 609. See also Marcus Aurelius, *Meditations* 5.10; 12.11.
[139] Marcus Aurelius, *Meditations* 11.20.
[140] Marcus Aurelius, *Meditations* 5.7.

3. Prayer in the Major Stoic Writers

Marcus does mentions prayer a few times. As noted above, he assumes one will pray, because the gods have power. However, the references to prayer that occur in his writings are mainly devices to help a person remember that Divine Reason rules the universe, so that one might accept one's fate willingly. This concept expresses itself in a "chillingly inhuman manner" at times:

> *Either the Gods have no power or they have power. If they have no power, why pray to them? But if they have power, why not rather pray that they should give thee freedom from fear of any of these things and from lust for any of these things and from grief at any of these things [rather] than that they should grant this or refuse that. For obviously if they can assist men at all, they can assist them in this...One prayers: How may I lie with that woman! Thou: How may I not lust to lie with her! Another: How may I be quit of that man! Thou: How may I not wish to be quit of him! Another: How may I not lose my little child! Thou: How may I not dread to lose him. In a word, give thy prayers this turn, and see what comes of it.*[141]

Often, his references to prayer read more like calls to meditate on the interdependence of the universe and of one's part in it rather than personal communication with the divine. "Meditate often on the intimate union and

---

[141] Marcus Aurelius, *Meditations* 4.40. See also 3.5-6; 4.14, 23.

mutual interdependence of all things in the Universe."[142] Still, at least in one instance, Marcus urges a more typical supplicatory prayer:

> *A Prayer of the Athenians: Rain, Rain, O dear Zeus, upon the corn-land of the Athenians, and their meads. Either pray not at all, or in this simple and frank fashion.*[143]

Similarly, in the *Sayings of Marcus Aurelius* (which may or may not be genuine), there is a prayer of request. It occurs during his telling of a story about the army of Emperor Antoninius. They were perishing of thirst, and the Emperor, raised both of his hands to heaven, writes Marcus, and prayed.

> *With this hand, wherewith I have taken away no life, have I implored Thee and besought the Giver of Life. And he so prevailed with God by his prayer that upon a clear sky there came up clouds bringing rain to his soldiers.*[144]

Marcus Aurelius' view of prayer and religion is far more practical and 'stoic' (in the modern sense of the word) than the previous Stoic writers. He reflects all the basic Stoic concepts of Divine Reason, Fate, Necessity, materialism, and Stoic pantheistic monism. His references to prayer are more like meditations on the subject. There is no sense of sin (except in wrong attitudes), no call for

---

[142]Marcus Aurelius, *Meditations* 9.40.
[143]Marcus Aurelius, *Meditations* 6.38. See also 6.23; 10.37.
[144]Marcus Aurelius, *Meditations* 5.7.

repentance, and no praise of the gods mentioned. Indeed, prayer for Marcus Aurelius seems primarily to function as a reminder that one is a cog in the great machine of the universe, ruled by Divine Reason.

Summary

Despite the varied views, personalities, and emphases of these six major Stoic writers, there are some basic ideals and teachings of religion and prayer which they all share. Stoic philosophy took seriously the dignity and majesty of God. The writers also all stress the obligation of humans to live in accordance with God, although they use the phrase "live in accordance with nature" (*secundum naturam*), most often. This is not surprising, since God and nature are so closely linked in their cosmology. The Stoics were basically monotheistic, and the philosophy does lean towards a surface pantheism—they spoke of God as Divine Reason which permeated the universe. There are some passages which even speak of God as identical to the universe, though usually there seems to be a distinction, at least twosome degree. Determinism is also a mainstay of Stoicism: some writers dealt with this in more detail and more systematically than others than others. All six Stoic writers appear to assume that a Stoic sage will offer petitionary prayers. Seneca attempts to address the apparent contradictions between determinism and petitionary prayer.

The language used in the prayers and references to prayer by these six writers often sound quite personal and pious, although it may be that this sense is more due to poetic purpose rather than theological understanding.

Finally, prayer is encouraged or assumed by all of these writers in terms of encouraging praise, petition, intercession, and thanksgivings. Vows and even confessions are indicated, though no prayers asking for forgiveness are found.

4. Stoic and New Testament Prayer

Having completed this brief and general overview of the teachings and references to prayer in these six major Stoic writers, we can now make some equally general comparisons between prayer in Stoicism and prayer in New Testament. Christian writers, just as Stoic writers, have different emphases and perhaps even varying beliefs about the content and purpose of prayer. It is also important to realize that any prayer found in the New Testament writings have their own context, and the writer had a specific purpose and situation in mind. Still, like the previous examination of Stoic prayer, the Christian writers share certain basic themes or characteristics. Therefore, the best way to proceed with a general comparison of Stoic and Christian prayer is to contrast those shared ideas or approaches. This chapter will do so by examining five topics that bear on prayer for both the Stoic and the Christian writers: God, eschatology, human nature and responsibility, ethics, and the practice and content of prayer itself.

God

There are a number of similarities between the way the Stoics and Christians think and write about God. In general, both believe that the deity is not merely an external object, but is a spiritual, inner, and invisible reality. This reality has ethical implications for humans, as a result, the nature of God calls humans to think and act in certain ways in order to fulfill their "created purpose" and to be in tune with the Universe (Stoics) or Creation (Christians). However, neither the New Testament writers nor first century Jewish writers would speak of themselves as "fragments of God," as do the Stoics. They might come close in believing that humans are created by God, that a part of God's spirit resides therein, but not that a spark exists within. (Later Christian Gnostics did, however, quite possibly through the influence of Stoic philosophy). Stoic philosophy held that human beings are what they are by nature, and it is their task to realize it and achieve their potential. It is by the work and power of a human that his or her destiny can be achieved—what someone might call "works-righteousness" from a Jewish or Christian point of view, though the Stoics would envision a "righteousness" in the same way. It would be "right reason," but not really a religious sanctification.[1] In contrast, the New Testament writers view the Spirit of God as an eschatological gift which is bestowed on God's followers, or among his community.

---

[1] See, for example, Marcus Aurelius, *Sayings* 12.

4. Stoic and New Testament Prayer

> *The foundation for salvation, according to Christianity, was in the life and death of Christ, and "upon this are based God's continuing dealings with humankind via preaching and the Holy Spirit (1Thess 1.4-6, 9-10; Gal 1.3-4; 1Cor 1.18-25, 30; 2Cor 5.17-21; Eph 1.3-14). In this respect Paul bears outward similarity with the Stoic view of God as immanent, though Paul never identified God with nature or the universe as the Stoa did. Thus Paul says "all things are from him and through him, and for him — a very Stoic-sounding phrase (see Rom 11.36; cf. Col 1.16). Yet God remains transcendent over the world he has created (1Cor 8.6; Col 1.15-19; Eph 4.6).*[2]

For Christians it is the church, rather than the universe, which is the "body." According to Greek philosophy, God was coeternal with matter, even thought he might be described as a craftsman or a shaper. Galen writes:

> *Moses' opinion differs greatly from the opinion of all...who among the Greeks have rightly investigated nature. To Moses it seems to be enough that God willed to create a cosmos and presently it was created...we, however, main-*

---

[2]Boring, 214.

> *tain on the contrary that certain things are impossible by nature, and these God would not even attempt to do.³*

Therefore, the Stoic God is limited within his power, and everything is periodically destroyed. There are no traces of anthropomorphism in their theology,[4] unlike in Jewish and Christian theology. Theistic language is found in Early and Late Stoa, along with the language of pantheism. But even in Cleanthes' "Hymn to Zeus," it is mere metaphor.[5]

The Stoics developed the idea that knowledge of God is possible through observation and the application of reason. Many commentators have noted a similar reference to natural theology written by Paul in Romans 1.19-20:

> *For what can be known about God is plain to them, because God has shown it to them. Ever since the creation of the world his eternal power and divine nature, invisible though they are, have been understood and seen through the things he has made.*

Yet the background for Paul's comment here is more likely drawn from Jewish wisdom sources, as seen in his use of the concept of the wrath of God just prior to this

---

[3]T. Paige, "Philosophy" in *Dictionary of Paul and his Letters*, ed. Gerald F. Hawthorne, Ralph P. Martin, and Daniel Reid, 713-718 (Leicester, England: Inter-Varsity Press, 1993), 716.
[4]Galen, *De Usu Partium* XI, 14 (III, pp. 905-906 K).
[5]

passage in Romans 1.18). It is highly unlikely, given Paul's context, and his theology taken as a whole from all of his extant writings, that he is reflecting the Stoic view. Even if there was any Stoic influence, it would most likely have been mediated through Jewish sources with which he was familiar from his extensive training as a Jewish lawyer.[6] Furthermore, and not surprisingly, the New Testament writers condemn cosmic religions of any kind, as does early Jewish literature of the time.[7]

Therefore, we see that there are some *general* similarities in the Stoic's view of God and in the Christian writer's view of God. But when we scratch the surface of both the theology and the specific content of those views, we find them to be based on quite different theologies and views of the Universe and of God. This is reflected in the prayers of both, as well.

Eschatology

Some of the Stoic writers examined above do not discuss eschatology at all, in contrast to many New Testament writers, where eschatology is an integral part of its theology and its ethics. The evolution of Stoicism into a primarily practical philosophy of ethics and morals means that the later Stoics had little or no use for eschatology.

---

[6] "As he puts it [Cleanthes], the Divine is better expressed through meter, song, and rhythm; prose is not an expression fitting the greatness of Divine things" (von Arnim, I *Fragment* 486). See pages 71 to 80 above.
[7] Paige, 717.

Prayer in the Ancient Stoic Tradition

Still, we can assume that they retained the belief of the earlier Stoics, which did focus on physics and cosmology, and included discussions of eschatology. The general belief of Stoics philosophers was that of a cyclical universe. At some point, the universe would end a great fiery cataclysm. Called the "Great Conflagration," a it resulted in a rebirth of a new Universe. Again, while there are sometimes similarities between the language used by the Stoics and the early Christian writers,[8] a deeper analysis their respective eschatological understandings is fundamentally different in both the grounds of the beliefs and the integration into the larger philosophy/religion. Prayer, for the Stoics, played no part in eschatology thinking. For Christians, a number of passages, including prayers, address the eschatological doctrines.[9]

There was a diversity of opinion among the Stoics concerning immortality, and the understanding of it changed as time marched on. Cleanthes wrote that all people survived until the Great Conflagration. Chrysippus, however, restricted morality only to the wise—his was a "limited immortality." Seneca adhered to the doctrine of the rebirth as cyclical and identical, and there are no deeper discussions about it in his existing writings (not surprising considering Seneca's focus on ethics and morals).

---

[8] See, for example, 2 Peter 3.10-13, which employs somewhat "Stoic-sounding" language about the "day of the Lord."

[9] For example, see Matt 8.11; 26.69; Mark 14.25; Luke 22.16; 18.30; Acts 7.55–56; Gal 1.4; Rom 8.18; 1 Cor 7.2; Phil 2.5-11; 1 Thess 4.

4. Stoic and New Testament Prayer

In contrast, the basic doctrine of the New Testament is not the immortality of the soul, but the resurrection of the body. This would probably have seemed ridiculous to the Greek Stoics, and likely to Roman Stoics as well. The general Greek view of matter and spirit would have almost precluded any such thing, and this explains, to a large degree, the problems that traditional Christianity had with Gnostic Christianity of the later centuries. Early Christianity, however, had received its understanding of matter and spirit from Hebrew and Jewish theology—there was not such a division between matter and spirit, and therefore no problem with a theology that suggested that matter could be redeemed. Eschatology in the New Testament is presented as deliverance and salvation, rather than merely a part of nature and beholden to Fate.

There was a broad stream in Hellenism, and therefore in Stoic philosophy, that affirmed that "all things are unfolding as they must." Benevolent God (or gods) had revealed the future for the good of humanity. Again, while similar language is found in the writings of the New Testament, there is a difference. The New Testament does include writings that discuss the issues of predestination, foreknowledge and revelation. Stoic writers often have a strict view of destiny: whatever happens to a person is destined to happen. Some Stoics, as shown above, do struggle with the idea of how to reconcile this strict view with a person's free will to choose to live by Reason and seek the best. By contrast, while Christian writers affirm that God has foreordained history, controls it, and sometimes reveals it, they do not seem to struggle with the idea. New Testament theology, if one can speak of such a thing in general, appears to take a less strict view than most (or all) Stoics. God has fore-ordained the major thrusts of history, and even some individual fates (or perhaps all?). Within that framework, God has power to alter and change course, all the while pursuing his will for the universe. C.K. Barrett has put it this way: the Stoic saying that "all things have been predestined by the 'gods' is a popular way of saying that all things happen in accordance with the universal reason."[10] The gods are aware of the future because of their point of view: they have no redemptive plan and purpose.[11]

Again, these ideas are reflected in the prayers of Stoics and of Christians. A cursory reading shows similarities, especially in there being some sort of 'divine plan for the universe, but a deeper investigations shows radical differences in terms of the power of God to alter history, and the purpose and meaning of how that history unfolds.

Human Nature and Responsibility

One of the basic Christian teaching of the New Testament writings is that humans are redeemed by grace. It's God's gift to humans, through his love and care of his creation. A Stoic philosopher, however, would say that it is the work of each human, through his own reason and work to conform to nature that brings fulfillment of the purpose of human life.

---

[10]Col, 2.28; Gal 4.8-10; Deut 4.19; Wis of Sol 13.2-3.
[11]Barrett, 69.

4. Stoic and New Testament Prayer

> *...the sage is god not because the highest god makes him a god, but rather through himself. There is no belief in "Thy will be done." Pascal saw this quite clearly, more clearly than the modern interpreters. The Stoic sage lack the virtue of humility. He knows of man's grandeur, not of his weakness.*[12]

While some of this overstates the fact (humility was a Stoic virtue), the basic argument is true. To the Stoics, "thy will be done" would referred to one's role in acquiescing to Fate, not a loyalty and acceptance of the fact that God has the best in mind for each human.

The Christian concept that a person should recognize their finite and minuscule role in the world, and submitting to God's will, would not be completely foreign to a Stoic philosopher. On the other hand, the Christian (and Jewish) call for one to recognize their own inability and neediness before God, that of a "broken and contrite heart," would be seen as evidence of a *lack* of faith to the Stoics.[13] Willpower and self-discipline are needed. They held up the accomplishment of the individual, though they did not usually call for imitation of a god or another sage. In contrast, Paul often encourages his readers to imitate him as he imitated Christ. Abraham Malherbe shows that ancient philosophers hesitated to call others to follow their examples, or even to use "contemporary

---

[12] See *Fragment* 1192 for Chrysippus' syllogism of the gods revealing future events. Compare Mt 3.7; Eph 6.14-17; Phil 2.12-13; see Boring, 48-49, 479, 481.

[13] Edelstein, 9.

worthies as paradigms."[14] Instead, seek virtue and "right reason," in order to train yourself to think and act as the universe is constructed.

Stoic philosophy asserted that humanity, as a whole, is one body.[15] Each member makes up a part of that one body. This concept is also found within Christianity, though it is the members of the community, those who are "in Christ," that make up the body—not all humans. The passages in the New Testament that employ this theme are strikingly consistent with Stoic thought and sometimes even in wording: "love thy neighbor," "law written in our hearts," "render unto Caesar the things that are Caesar's, render unto God the things that are God's," "what shall it profit a man to gain the whole world and lose his soul?" This has led some scholar to suggest a direct dependence, yet, again, the similarities appear to be drawn from common contemporary concepts rather than one drawing on the others. The are difference as well, for when Stoics speak of "brotherhood," they are often actually speaking of the wise: their contempt for the average man is apparent.[16] Though Christian writers are speaking of the body as members of the larger Chris-

---

[14] Leonard Alston, *Stoic and Christian in the Second Century* (New York: Longman, Green and Co., 1906), 113.

[15] Malherbe, 57. See also G.C. Fiske, *Lucilius and Horace: A Study in Classical Theory of Imitation.* University of Wisconsin Studied in Language and Literature 7 (Madison: University of Wisconsin Press, 1970), 159-162.

[16] Cicero, *De Finibus* 3.63; Epictetus, *Discourses* 1.13.3-4; Arnim, III *Fragment* 450.

4. Stoic and New Testament Prayer

tian community, they do not have contempt for non-believers. The prayers reflect this, for Stoic prayer tends to be focus on the individual and guidance, whereas Christian prayer often offers prayers for others—even non-believers.

Stoic philosophers taught the ultimate goal of life was happiness through living in accordance with nature. Christian writers (see the Sermon on the Mount, for example) suggests that happiness comes because of the certainty that God will take care of his people. In Stoicism, happiness is primarily something to be attained through one's one will and discipline; in Christianity, it is an attitude to be adopted because God is in control of history. Still, there is a similar here in that both stress acceptance of the events that come one's way, good or ill. The contrast is found in that the Stoic way is that of individual discovery and work; the Christian way focuses more on discovering and accepting God's grace in spite of one's weaknesses. The respective attitudes are found within the prayers of each as well: the language used is often similar, but the detail and the reasons are different in prayers which address contentment or happiness.

The theme of "suffering" is found in some Stoic writings; it is a common theme in the New Testament.[17] Seneca advised wealthy Stoics to welcome minor discomforts, in order to prepare for more serious hardships. Again, this virtue for Stoics lies in personal discipline for one's own betterment. In the New Testament however,

---

[17]This is especially apparent in the writings of Marcus Aurelius. See *Meditations* 4.48, 50; 5.10; 6.27; 7.62, 70; 8.44, 53; 9.18, 27; 10.19; etc.

suffering is linked to imitation of Christ and to piety.[18] One suffers on behalf of others (sacrifices for others), because that is what Christ did. Although Paul's language of imitative suffering may resemble many of Seneca's statements (as well as that of the Socratic school), the driving force behind the Stoic view of suffering was not due to a Cross or a Savior.[19] As a Stoic, one suffered for one's own benefit; as a Christian, one suffered for the benefit of others or to imitate God's character. The prayers in both reflect this difference—similar in language, different in grounds.

Ethics

It is in this area that we find some of the closest parallels with Christianity, leading some (mostly earlier scholars) to suggest that Stoic morality was infused into Christianity.[20] Teachings about how to treat others, personal responsibility, purity, and high moral standards are all primary in both Christianity and Stoicism. William Vorster has shown that a comparison of the writings of the Stoics and Christians concerning "happiness" through ethical behavior display remarkable similarities.[21] The similari-

---

[18] Possibly due to his closeness to Nero's court and its fickleness. See Shelton, 435.
[19] See 1 Tim 6.6-8, 12.
[20] Markus Barth, "Traditions in Ephesians," *New Testament Studies* (1984), 18.
[21] See Edelstein, 96.

4. Stoic and New Testament Prayer

ties between Stoic language and the ethics language employed by Paul of Tarsus have been long noted, especially similarities with Seneca's writings.[22] Sevenster suggests that these similarities are only formal, for beneath the language are very different concepts. It is possible, however, that Paul was consciously reworking Stoic concepts in light of Christian theology.[23] So *autarkeia* (self-sufficiency) in 2 Corinthians 9.8 and *autarkes (*self-sufficient) in Philippians 4.11, Paul uses the terms in order to stress that a Christian can be content because God has supplied all they need. Those same terms are technical terms in Stoic and Cynic thought, used to express the contentment of the wise man with a "life in accord with nature" achieved by the rejection of material goods. The Stoic wise becomes a heroic figure rising above the gods in independence. Paul sees these terms as reflecting a dependent existence flowing from the grace of God. Prayers in each reflect those substantive and purposive differences.

In some passages, Paul incorporates the stylistic form of diatribe, a form used in popular philosophic teaching; the Stoics were especially fond of its use. In Paul's writings, the model is mainly found in catalogues of vices,[24]

---

[22] William S. Vorster, "Stoics and Early Christians on Blessedness" in *Greeks, Romans, and Christians,* eds. David L. Balch, Everett Ferguson, and Wayne A. Meeks, 38-51 (Philadelphia: Fortress, 1990), 50.

[23] See Rom 1.19-20, 26; 11.36; 12.1; 1 Cor 3.21-23; 6.12; 7.31; 9.1,19; 12.12-27; Col 1.16; Eph 4.6, 5.22-6.9.

[24] See Paige, 717.

catalogues of virtues,[25] the so-called *Haustafeln*[26] (literally "household codes") and *Peristasenkataloge*.[27] We can again point to similarities in language and differences of ground between Stoic and Christian teachings, yet those difference are much less pronounced in ethical teachings. Schmeller points out that, although ethics are a function of the intellect in Stoicism, and a function of existence in Christianity, the difference is difficult to detect when Stoic ethics become popular and included strong religious elements.[28] Additionally, *Haustafeln* in Stoicism are directed at husbands and fathers, but in Paul they are also directed at women, children, and slaves.

Likewise, the concepts of "spirit" and "flesh" do not correspond exactly in Paul and Stoicism, despite similar language. The dualistic tension and mutual existence of soul and body in Stoicism is refuted by the statement that God created all things.[29] The intimate connection between matter and spirit in Judaism and Christianity was reject by most Greek philosophy.

It becomes obvious that the ethics of Stoicism are different that those of Christianity because they differ in the broader framework in which they were conceptualized, in spite of strong linguistic similarities.

---

[25] Rom 1.29-31; 13.13; 1 Cor 5.10-11; 6.9-10; 2 Cor 12.20; Gal 5.19-21; Eph 4.31, 5.3-5; Col 3.5, 8.
[26] Gal 5.22-23; Phil 4.8; Col 3.12; 1 Tim 6.11; 2 Peter 1.5-7.
[27] Eph 5.22-6.9; Col 3.18-4.1; 1 Pet 2.18-3.7.
[28] See 1 Cor 4.10-13; 2 Cor 4.8-12, 6.4-10, 11.23-29, 12.10.
[29] Schmeller, 213.

4. Stoic and New Testament Prayer

> *...while in Stoicism Socrates is the radiant example of ethical conduct (including the readiness to suffer), in Ephesians Jesus Christ, through his sacrificial death, is the sacrament of ethics. Socrates lived on in the memory and teaching of the Stoics; Jesus Christ was raised from the dead and given responsibility and rule over all persons and all things.*[30]

Lightfoot may have put it best when he said that those who see the gospel as a series of moral precepts will see all sorts of parallels to pagan antiquity, and Stoicism in particular. "But the mere ethical teachings, however important, is the least important, because it is the least distinctive part of Christianity."[31] It is the theology and philosophy of Judaism and Christianity, from which those ethics flow, that is the core meaning of the faith. This stands in stark contrast to Stoic philosophy's ground of ethics. Not surprisingly, the prayers which address ethical behavior in both systems reflect these similarities on the surface, and differences in substance.

Prayer

As we have already seen in the numerous citations of Stoic prayer and references to prayer, there are similarities of language with New Testament prayer, but differences in content, grounds, and presuppositions. Once we

---

[30]Eph 3.9.
[31]Barth, 19. See also Eph 1.19-23; cf. 1.10; 4.8-10.

understand the basic cosmology and theology/philosophy because each, this is not surprising. Both Stoic popular philosophy and the genesis of Christianity out of first century Judaism were roughly contemporaneous. The Greco-Roman social, political, and religio-philosophical world out of which they both grew would influence the language of each in a similar fashion. Methods of teaching, in that same cultural milieu, would presumably draw on the same forms, concepts, language, and teaching techniques. But the underlying understandings of the universe, of the purpose of life, and of the gods, would make the grounds and purpose of prayer different.

Paul assumes prayer as a matter of course, and that it is meaningful and important. Stoic writers also seem to assume prayer has a purpose in life, and the gods should not be ignored, yet the role of prayer in Stoicism seems more of a secondary issues than in Christianity. Paul exhorts his readers to pray constantly,[32] and teaches them that the Spirit comes to their aid in prayer.[33] Stoics suggest prayer should be offered, but do not engage in strong exhortation of the practice, and they certainly do not suggest that any spirit of the gods might assist them in prayer, in spite of their belief that a divine spark resides in all humans. Paul took for granted that prayers would be heard; the Stoic writers may take the same view, though the depiction of God in Stoic writings is much less personal and reflects a divine indifference (or perhaps distance) from human plight.

---

[32] See Col 1.3; 1 Cor 1.4; Phil 1.9; Col 1.9; 1 Thess 1.2; 2 Thess 1.3, 11; Phlm 4 for a few examples.

[33] 1 Thess 5.17.

4. Stoic and New Testament Prayer

As for the forms of prayer, thanksgiving and praise are found in both, and are much alike in Paul and in the Stoics (though prayers of thanksgiving and praise occur less often in Stoic writings than in Christian writing). The Stoic prayers tend to focus more on God as Divine Reason, giving structure to the universe, while Christian writings describe thanksgiving and praise due to God because he is creator and sustainer of the universe, and closely involved in the life of humans. The content of Paul's numerous thanksgivings stand in contrast to Stoic indifference: Christians can be hurt, disappointed, confused, or defeated, but never driven to total despair.[34] Stoics suggest that it is personal discipline in acceptance of those things that will keep one from despair.

Intercessions and supplications are also quite common in Christian prayer, but less so in Stoic prayer. Paul, specially, makes constant references to prayers of supplication and intercessions,[35] both offering prayers for his readers and others, as well as encouraging them to engage in such prayers. Little of this is found in Stoic writings—again, perhaps, because the focus of a Stoic was on striving to live within the divine structure of the universe rather than asking God to intervene.

Prayers of confession of common in the Christian writings, but not found in Stoic writers. This is not surprising, because the practice of confession to God in Christianity flows from the specifics of Judeo-Christian theology itself: humans are in need of redemption because of

---

[34] Rom 8.26.
[35] Lightfoot, 328.

sin, and call on God to forgive and redeem. Stoic philosophy had no such concept of sin—sin was merely error in personal virtue and discipline). The correction for error was an understanding of the structure of the universe and Divine Reason, and from that knowledge could come personal discipline to live in accordance with it. Therefore, confession had no role, except perhaps in the sense of self-confession in order to bring one's errors to light in order to correct them.

The strong connections between Stoic prayer and Christian prayer are primarily found in areas where both praise God, and in prayers that encourage ethical behavior. But the purpose, grounds, and philosophical/theological content of prayer is quite different between the two systems, in almost every way.

Sevenster sums up the characteristic difference between Stoic prayer and Christian prayer by contrasting Seneca's view of prayer and Paul's view of prayer:

> *Paul's way of thinking and living revolves around his unshakable belief in the God and Father of Jesus Christ, which inevitably causes him to see prayer against the background of a living God's proclamation of salvation. Seneca is obliged to argue about prayer in terms of his conception of God, and to incorporate it as best he can in a local train of thought, which is in harmony with an articulate theory of the universe.*[36]

---

[36] See 2 Cor 4.8-11.

5. Summary and Conclusions

This brief and general survey demonstrates that there are a remarkable number of similarities between Stoic prayer and New Testament prayer, especially in style and language. Yet their respective presuppositions about God, humanity, and the relationship between the two are quite different. For the Stoic, Fate inevitably marches on and one cannot change that through prayer. Still, teach the Stoics, one should pray to the gods because it would be irrational not to join in with their will. The New Testament writers, however, imply that God hears prayer, and that prayer can and does have an effect.

The Stoics stress self-reliance, because humans are a part of the Divine Reason of the universe, capable of lifting themselves up to the level of the gods through their own discipline and use of reason. Although God is sometimes referred to in personal terms, those terms appear to be merely poetic language and not intended to represent a truly personal deity. The New Testament writers, on the other hand, speak of God using the Jewish word *abba*, a parent, who desires a personal, intimate relationship with his children. This relationship is quite different from that found in Stoicism. The Stoic writers stress self-reliance; the New Testament writers stress reliance on God.

Much of the language, attitude, and ethical stances in Stoic thought and prayer are similar to those found in the New Testament. Did Stoic thought and prayer affect the writers of the New Testament? Or is it possible, as some have suggested, that the early Christians had an effect on the later Stoics? The latter is unlikely,[1] although E.V. Arnold presents a convincing model which describes how a Stoic might have responded to the narrative about Jesus and the Christian message.[2] Lightfoot suggests that Seneca may have had some knowledge of Christianity.[3]

It is more likely, however, that Stoic terminology and moral terms were available in the contemporary culture and appropriated by the New Testament writers: these concepts and ideas were "in the air" for anyone to appropriate as part of the language of the time. They were a manner of communicating. One might think of the focus of the term "family values" in the US political atmosphere of the 1980s and 1990s. The term was used by political parties and others, but meaning different things: conservatives might use it to express traditional, long-held social values; progressives might use it to mean a more open, progressive acceptance of non-traditional family structures. The Christian and the Stoics may very well have been using the same terminology to express similar concepts, with different core beliefs and suppositions.

---

[1] Sevenster, 52.
[2] See Winckler, *Der Stoicismus eine Wurzel des Christenthums* (1878), 5–14.
[3] See Arnold, 411–412.

5. Summary and Conclusions

For example, the Prologue of the Fourth Gospel uses language that is strikingly similar to Stoic thought.[4] Tarsus was a center of Hellenistic philosophy of every kind, and especially Stoicism.[5] It is possible that Paul, having grown up and been educated in Tarsus, had studied Stoicism. At the least, he had encountered their teachings, since he quite obviously uses some their language, and even quotes one of their poets in Acts (if we assume the historical reliability of the Acts passage).[6] Malherbe believes that Paul "deftly situated himself in the philosophical landscape."[7] Paul's teaching was positive and dogmatic, much like the Stoics. He used Stoic themes, but redefined them.

The best understanding is that Christian prayer flourished in the same Greco-Roman religious and social milieux as Stoicism, rather than assuming that one had a direct effect on the other. Christians were certainly critical of the materialism of the Stoic psychology and theology, and the absence of a transcendent Creator. After all, to reach a Greco-Roman audience with a message that grew out of an old and established religion from the ancient near east (Judaism), would require speaking in a language that would make sense to those Greeks and Romans.

---

[4] John 1.1–18.
[5] Lightfoot, 305.
[6] Acts 17.28.
[7] Arnold, 414; Lightfoot, 306; Paige, 714; see also Juvenal, *Satires* 3.117–118.

> *...they had no alternative but to take material where it lay at hand in the thought of the pagans, and they found as much that was suitable among the Stoics as among the Platonists. Often, it must be admitted, they modified the meaning of the vocabulary they took over.*[8]

Still, a lot of that language could be assimilated without change: the world is the work of God, it is a harmonious unity, determined by Providence, designed for the benefit of man. Some New Testament passages drift far closer to actual Stoic thought than others, especially the later letters[9]—perhaps in need of reaching a larger Greco-Roman audience, or perhaps under a greater and more long-term influence of that culture upon Christianity. Yet the presuppositions about God, humanity, and their relationships are not the same in the New Testament as those concepts as found in Stoicism. For the New Testament writers, these understandings grew out of the Old Testament and Second Temple Judaism.

In summary, prayer in the New Testament shares a number of similarities in style, language, and vocabulary with Stoicism—especially late Stoicism. Early Christian writers may have appropriated some Stoic language and redefined in light of Christian theology. A more detailed study, comparing all of the prayers of the New Testament with all of the existing Stoic prayers from the period, would perhaps suggest different conclusions. It could certainly present a more nuanced picture of prayer in the

---

[8]Malherbe, 7.
[9]Sandback, 177.

5. Summary and Conclusions

two systems. However, in light of the present study, such an investigation would likely affirm that the content of Christian prayer is essentially Jewish, while often cloaked in the words, style, and imagery of Hellenistic thought as exemplified in Stoic prayers.

Select Bibliography

Ahroni, Reuben. "Biblical and other studies in memory of S. D. Goitein." *Hebrew Annual Review* 9 (1985): 1-381.

Alston, Leonard. *Stoic and Christian in the Second Century*. New York: Longman, Green and Co., 1906.

Annas, Julia. "Stoicism." In *The Oxford Classical Dictionary*, 3rd edition, ed. Simon Hornblower, and Antony Spawforth, 1640. New York: Oxford University Press, 1996.

Armstrong, Arthur H., ed. *Classical Mediterranean Spirituality: Egyptian, Greek, Roman*. World Spirituality, 15. New York, 1986.

Arnold, E.V. *Roman Stoicism*. Cambridge, 1911.

Attridge, Harold W. "The philosophical critique of religion under the early empire." In *Principat 16/1. Aufstieg und Niedergang der römischen Welt*, ed. W. Haase, 45-78. New York: De Gruyter, 1978.

Aurelius, Marcus. *Meditations*. Cambridge, MA: Harvard University Press, 1916, 1994.

Balch, David L. "The Areopagus Speech: An Appeal to the Stoic Historian Posidonius against Later Stoics and the Epicureans." In *Greeks, Romans, and Christians*. ed. David L, Everett Ferguson, and Wayne A. Meeks Balch, 52-79. Philadelphia: Fortress, 1990.

Barclay, William. "Hellenistic thought in New Testament Times: the Stoics." *Expository Times* 72 (1961): 164-166; 200-203; 227-230; 258-261; 291-294.

Barrett, C.K., ed. *The New Testament Background: Writings from Ancient Greece and the Roman Empire That Illuminate Christian Writings.* San Francisco: Harper & Rowe, 1956, 1987.

Barth, Markus. "Traditions in Ephesians." *New Testament Studies* (1984): 3-25.

Blakeney, E.H. *The Hymn of Cleanthes.* London, 1921.

Boring, M. Eugene, Klaus Berger, and Carsten Colpe, ed. *Hellenistic Commentary to the New Testament.* Nashville: Abingdon Press, 1995.

Buffière, F. Héraclite, *Allégories d'Homère.* Paris, 1963.

Cassidy, William. "Cleanthes — Hymn to Zeus." In *Prayer from Alexander to Constantine: A Critical Anthology*, ed. Mark Kiley, et. al., 133-138. New York: Routledge, 1997.

Colish, Marcia L. "Stoicism and the New Testament: An Essay in Historiography." In *Aufstieg und Niedergang der römischen Welt, Principat*, 26.1, ed. H., and W. Haase Temporini, 334-379. Berlin, 1992.

Colish, Marcia L. *The Stoic Tradition: From Antiquity to the Middle Ages.* 2 Vols.. Leiden: E.J. Brill, 1985-1990.

Des Places, Edouard. "La priäre des philosophes grecs." *Gregorianum* 41 (1960): 253-272.

Doignon, Jean. "Ordre du monde, connaissance de Dieu et ignorance de soi chez Hilaire de Poitiers." *Revue des Sciences Philosophiques et Théologiques* 60 (1976): 565-578.

Select Bibliography

Dorandi, Tiziano. "Per la cronologia dei filosofi ellenistici: Cleante e Crantore." In *Proceedings of the XIXth International Congress of Papyrology, Cairo, 2-9 September 1989*, ed. A. El-Mosalamy, 491-502. Cairo: Ain Shams University, Center of Papyrological Studies, 1992.

Edelstein, Ludwig. *The Meaning of Stoicism*. Cambridge, 1966.

Epictetus, *Discourses and Enchiridion*. Cambridge, MA: Harvard University Press, 1925, 1995.

Ferguson, Everett. *Backgrounds of Early Christianity*. Eerdmans: Grand Rapids, Michigan, 1993.

Fischel, Henry A. *Essays in Greco-Roman and related Talmudic literature*. The Library of Biblical Studies. New York, 1977.

Fiske, G.C. *Lucilius and Horace: A Study in Classical Theory of Imitation*. University of Wisconsin Studied in Language and Literature 7. Madison: University of Wisconsin Press, 1970.

Fitzgerald, John T. "Philodemus and the Papyri from Herculaneum." In *Philodemus and the New Testament World Philosophy*, ed. By John T. Firzgerald, et al. Leiden: Brill, 2004.

Glei, Reinhold. "Der Zeushymnus des Kleanthes." In *'Ihr alle aber seid Brüder': Festschrift fur A. Th. Khoury zum 60. Geburtstag*. Wurzburger Forschungen zur Missions- und Religionswissenschaft. Religionswissenschaftliche Studien 14, ed. L. Hagemann, et. al., 577-597. Wurzburg: Echter, 1990.

Glover, T. R. *The Conflict of Religions in the Early Roman Empire*. London: Methuen, 1932.

Gould, Josiah B. *The Philosophy of Chrysippus*. Albany: State University of New York Press, 1970.

Grant, F. C. *Hellenistic Religions*. New York, 1953.
Hadas, M. *The Stoic Philosophy of Seneca*. New York, 1968.
Hamman, Adalbert "La prière chrétienne et la prière païenne, forms et différences." In *Aufstieg und Niedergang der römischen Welt, Principat, 31.2*, ed. H., and W. Haase Temporini, 1190-1243. Berlin, 1992.
Herrmann, Léon. *Sénèque et les premiers chrétiens*. Brussels: Latomus, 1979.
Hobein, H. "Stoa." In *Real-Encyclopädie der classischen Altertumswissenschaft*, ed. A. Pauly, and G. Wissowa, 1-47. Stuttgart, 1839-.
Laertius, Diogenes. *Lives of Eminent Philosophers*. Volume 2. Loeb Classical Library. Cambridge, MA: Harvard University Press, 1925, 1958.
Lauer, Simon. "Der Zeushymnus des Kleanthes." In *Das Vaterunser*, ed. M. Brocke, 156-162. , 1974.
Lightfoot, J.B. *Saint Paul's Epistle to the Philippians*. London, repr. Grand Rapids, 1953, 1913.
Long, A.A, and D.N. Sedley. *The Hellenistic Philosophers. Volume 1: Translations of the Principle Sources, with Philosophical Commentary*. Cambridge: Cambridge University Press, 1987.
Long, A.A, and D.N. Sedley. *The Hellenistic Philosophers. Volume 2: Greek and Latin Texts with Notes and Bibliography*. Cambridge: Cambridge University Press, 1987.
Long, A. A., ed. *Problems in Stoicism*. London, 1971.
Long, A.A. "Aristotle's Legacy to Stoic Ethics." *Bulletin of the Institute of Classical Studies* 15 (1968): 72-85.
Long, A.A. *Hellenistic Philosophy: Stoics, Epicureans, Skeptics*. New York: Charles Scribner's Sons, 1974.

Long, A.A. "Heraclitus and Stoicism," in *Stoic Studies*. Cambridge: Cambridge University Press, 1996.

Long, A.A. *Stoic Studies*. Cambridge: Cambridge University Press, 1996.

Lutz, C. E. *Musonius Rufus, "The Roman Socrates."* Yale Classical Series 10. New Haven: Yale University Press, 1947.

Malherbe, Abraham. *Paul and the Popular Philosophers*. Philadelphia: Fortress, 1989.

Mansfeld, J. "Providence and the destruction of the universe in early Stoic thought, with some remarks on the 'mysteries of philosophy'." In *Studies in Hellenistic Religions*, ed. M. Vermaseren, 129-188. Leiden: Brill, 1979.

Martin, Ralph P. *New Testament Foundations: A Guide for Christian Students*. Volume 2, The Acts, The Letters, The Apocalypse. Grand Rapids, Michigan: Eerdmans: , 1978, 1994.

McDowell, Markus. *Prayers of Jewish Women: Studies of Patterns of Prayer in the Second Temple Period*. Wissenschaftliche Untersuchungen Zum Neuen Testament-2 Reihe, volume 211. Tübingen: Mohr Siebeck, 2006.

Murray, Gilbert. *Stoic, Christian and Humanist*. London, C. A. Watts & Co. ltd., 1940.

Nilsson, N. "Pagan Divine Service in Late Antiquity." *Harvard Theological Review* 38 (1954): 63-69.

Oates, W. J. *The Stoic and Epicurean Philosophers*. New York, 1957.

Paige, T. "Philosophy." In *Dictionary of Paul and his Letters*, ed. Gerald F. Hawthorne, Ralph P. Martin, and Daniel Reid, 713-718. Leicester, England: InterVarsity Press, 1993.

Pépin, Jean. "Cosmic piety." In *Classical Mediterranean Spirituality: Egyptian, Greek, Roman*, ed. A.H. Armstrong, 408-435. New York: Crossroad, 1986.

Pépin, Jean. Mythe et allégorie. Les origines grecques et les contestations judó-chrétiennes, Philosophe de l'esprit. Paris, 1958.

Pinset, John. "Roman Piety." In *Classical Mediterranean spirituality: Egyptian, Greek, Roman*, ed. A. H. Armstrong, 154-194. New York: Crossroad, 1986.

Pohlenz, Max. *Paulus und die Stoa*. Zeitschrift für die Neutestamentliche Wissenschaft und die Kunde der Alteren Kirche 42. Darmstadt: Wissenschaftliche Buchgesellschaft, 1949.

Reesor, Margaret E. "Fate and Possibility in Early Stoic Philosophy." *Phoenix* 19, 1965: 285-297.

Reesor, Margaret E. "Necessity and Fate in Stoic Philosophy." In *The Stoics*. Major Thinkers Series 1, ed. J. M. Rist, 187-202. Berkeley: University of California Press, 1978.

Rist, J.M. *Stoic Philosophy*. London, 1975.

Robert, L. "Dans un maison d'Ephèse: Un serpent et un chiffre." *Comptes rendus de l'Académue des inscriptions et belles-lettres* (1982): 126-132.

Rocca-Serra, Guillaume. "Les philosophes stoäciens et le syncrétisme." In *Syncrétismes dans les Religions Grecque*, ed. S. Wikander, 15-24. Paris: Paris Universitie de France, 1973.

Saffrey, H. D. "The Piety and Prayers of Ordinary Men and Women in Late Antiquity." In *Classical Mediterranean Spirituality: Egyptian, Greek, Roman*, ed. A. H. Armstrong, 195-213. New York: Crossroad, 1986.

Sandbach, F.H. *The Stoics*. London, 1975.

Schmekel, August. *Die Philosophie der mittleren Stoa in ihrem geschichtlichen Zusammenhange*. Berlin: Weidmann, 1892.

Schmeller, Thomas. "Stoics, Stoicism." In *Anchor Bible Dictionary*, Volume 6, ed. David Noel Freedman, 210-214. New York: Doubleday, 1992.

Sevenster, J. N. *Paul and Seneca*. Supplements to Novum Testamentum. Leiden: E. J. Brill, 1961.

Sharp, Douglas S. *Epictetus and the New Testament*. London: Charles H. Kelly, 1914.

Shelton, Jo-Ann. *As the Romans Did: A Sourcebook in Roman Social History*. Oxford: Oxford University Press, 1988.

Sørensen, Villy. *Seneca: The Humanist at the Court of Nero*. Chicago: University of Chicago Press, 1984.

Stern, M. *Greek and Latin Authors on Jews and Judaism, From Herodotus to Plutarch*. Jerusalem, 1974.

Stevenson, Richard Taylor. "Twice on Mars' Hill." *Methodist Review* 76 (1894): 353-368.

Stough, Charlotte. "Stoic Determinism and Moral Responsibility." In *The Stoics*. Major Thinkers Series 1, ed. J. M. Rist, 203-231. Berkeley: University of California Press, 1978.

Super, Charles W. *Between Heathenism and Christianity*. Chicago: Fleming H. Revell Company, 1899.

Turcan, R. *Sénèca et les religions orientales*. Coll. Latomus 91. Bruxelles, 1967.

van der Horst, P. W. "Cornutus and the New Testament." *Novum Testamentum* 23 (1981): 165-172.

van Geytenbeek, A.C. *Musonius Rufus and Greek Diatribe*. Assen: Van Gorcum, 1963.

Vorster, William S. "Stoics and Early Christians on Blessedness." In *Greeks, Romans, and Christians*, ed. David L. Balch, Everett Ferguson, and Wayne A. Meeks , 38-51. Philadelphia: Fortress, 1990.

Welles, C. Bradford. *Greece and Rome*. New Haven, 1965.

Wenley, R.M. *Stoicism and its Influence*. New York, 1963.

Williams, David J. *1 and 2 Thessalonians*, New International Biblical Commentary. Peabody, Mass: Hendrickson Publishers, 1992.

Wu, Julie Lee. "Paul's Use of Prayer Speech in his Chief Epistles: Backgrounds and Significance." Ph.D. Diss., Fuller Theological Seminary, School of Theology, 1991.

Zeller, E. *Stoics, Epicureans, and Sceptics*. New York, 1962.

ABOUT THE AUTHOR

Markus McDowell holds a Ph.D. in Theology from Fuller Theological Seminary and a law degree from the University of London. He is a researcher and a writer, and has taught and lectured at various universities in the US, Europe, and the UK. He is the author of *Prayers of Jewish Women: Studies of Patterns of Prayer in the Second Temple Period*, published by Mohr Siebeck in 2006, as well as other works on prayer in the ancient world.

Website: http://markusmcdowell.com

Facebook: https://www.facebook.com/pages/Markus-McDowell/1445108122445923

www.ingramcontent.com/pod-product-compliance
Lightning Source LLC
Chambersburg PA
CBHW021441080526
44588CB00009B/625